Robert Irwin

Real Estate
Education Company
® a division of Dearborn Financial Publishing, Inc.

While a great deal of care has been taken to provide accurate and current information, the ideas, suggestions, general principles and conclusions presented in this text are subject to local, state and federal laws and regulations, court cases and any revisions of same. The reader is thus urged to consult legal counsel regarding any points of law—this publication should not be used as a substitute for competent legal advice.

Acquisitions Editor: Christine E. Litavsky
Managing Editor: Jack Kiburz
Editorial Assistant: Stephanie C. Schmidt
Interior Design: Elizandro Carrington
Cover Design: S. Laird Jenkins Corporation

Published by Real Estate Education Company,
a division of Dearborn Financial Publishing, Inc.

Printed in the United States of America

95 96 97 10 9 8 7 6 5 4 3 2 1

Library of Congress Cataloging-in-Publication Data

Irwin, Robert, 1941-
    Buy your first home / by Robert Irwin.
      p.   cm.
    Includes index.
    ISBN 0-7931-1293-1 (pbk.)
    I. House buying   I. Title
HD 1379.I642 1995
649'.12—dc20   94-46495
                                                           CIP

CONTENTS

BUY YOUR
FIRST HOME!

Deciding to Purchase

CHAPTER

Buying a home for the first time—or for the first time in a long while —can be an exciting adventure, as well as a scary one. There are plenty of things to worry about: Will you pay too much? Are you choosing the right neighborhood? Will you really like the house? Can you afford the payments?

On the other hand, there's also the pleasure of finally participating in the American dream of owning a home of your own. No more having to be quiet because other tenants might complain. No more having to fight for a parking spot nearby. No more dealing with land-lords.

And it can be lots of fun to have agents escort you around to different locations or to check out builders' new models. If you used to wonder what to do on a weekend, participating in the truly American custom of house-hunting will fill your time with delight as well as a certain amount of frustration.

You're Not Alone!

Every year nearly two million Americans hunt for and purchase their first home. Nearly three-quarters of your colleagues in this endeavor are married. Most have spent between three and five years saving up the down payment (many will be helped out by parents or relatives). Over two-thirds will buy a single-family house, with the remainder buying townhomes or condos.

All of these homebuyers are as diverse as the ethnic and cultural variety of this country. And while the homes they choose will include co-ops in New York, ranch styles in California, prairie models in Minnesota, condos in Florida and everything you can imagine in between, what they all have in common with you is that the home-purchasing experience is a new one.

Chances are that you will be thrust into the world of real estate investing (after all, a home is usually the biggest investment most people ever make), home financing and deal making for the first time. And it's very easy to quickly feel that you're in over your head.

Are They Ganging Up on Me?

When that real estate agent starts asking if you want "fixed rate" or an "ARM with no negative," or whether you prefer a "fixer-upper" or a house with "curb appeal," it's easy to get just a little intimidated. Then when you're asked to come up with a deposit check of $1,000 or more and to sign a contract that's often four or five pages long filled with legalese no one can understand, it's enough to make you want to throw in the towel and go back to the simple life of renting, where you can call the management when the toilet's stopped up!

JUST A LITTLE HELP

Rest assured that the vast majority of first-time homebuyers do quickly pick up the new vocabulary and the techniques needed to successfully deal with agents and sellers. You'll also become adept at home inspections and even at handling the paperwork. But it helps to have a bit of guidance along the way, and that's where this book comes in.

Buy Your First Home! was written after consulting with many, many new buyers and experienced brokers to determine those areas that are most often of concern. As result, with this book you'll

- learn how to find the best locations;

- determine exactly how much you can afford;

- experience the relief of finally realizing what you truly want in a home;

- compare the different costs and lifestyles of condos, co-ops and townhouses versus a single-family residence;

- find out about the special types of financing available just for first-time homebuyers (as little as 5 percent down or less!);

- discover how much to offer on any property and how big a deposit check to write;

- come to understand the sales agreement;

- begin to negotiate terms and conditions like a pro;

- know what's expected of you at closing and how to keep from being cheated; and

- figure the best way to save on your taxes.

In short, *Buy Your First Home!* offers you the simple tools you need to master buying your new home. It's all here, quick and easy.

Don't worry, you won't have to spend a lot of time burrowing in this book. When a question comes up, though, you'll know exactly where to turn to find a practical answer that should help.

MAKING THE PURCHASE DECISION

But first things first. Should you really buy a home, or should you continue to rent? Buying a home has both advantages and negatives, and it's important to consider both sides before making the leap.

When you purchase, you are taking on the responsibilities of ownership. Many of these are financial. You'll now have to pay the following:

- Mortgage(s)

- Taxes

- Insurance

- Maintenance

- Homeowners' fees for condo, co-op or association

- All utilities

With careful planning, you'll have it all worked out so that you can afford to meet these obligations without breaking your checkbook. But also keep in mind that with a house, you can't as easily pick up and move. There's no giving the landlord 30 days' notice. If you get a job in a new area or you simply decide you want to try living elsewhere, you'll need to sell your home (which could take as long as half a year or more, plus be costly) or, if you can't or don't want to sell, you'll have to rent it out—which now puts *you* in the position of being a landlord with a whole new list of responsibilities.

No, I'm not trying to scare you off, but it's important to understand the baggage that goes along with a house. Of course, millions of people each year feel it's all worthwhile. That's because the advantages of home ownership are both personal and financial.

On the personal side, there's the very real pleasure of being master of your castle. You can put a nail in the wall to hang a picture without worrying that you might not get all your cleaning deposit back. If you want a pet, you don't have to be concerned about what the neighbor next door will say. In short, there's a kind of freedom that comes with home ownership that tenants never get to experience.

In addition, there are financial rewards. You get to deduct (in most cases) all your mortgage interest and your taxes. (That helps make the big monthly payments more bearable; remember, residential rent is not deductible.) In addition, when you sell, you can often defer your gain from immediate taxation by rolling it over into a more expensive home. And when you reach the age of 55, you may be eligible for a big "gift" from Uncle Sam—you may not have to pay taxes on up to $125,000 of the profit on the sale of your home. If you have an office at home, you may even be able to take a deduction for it.

Finally, there's the profit motive. Although home prices fell in most parts of the country at the beginning of the 1990s, historically they have been an excellent investment. Even at the bottom of the recent market, most homes were selling for three to four times their value of 20 years earlier. And once again, the opportunity for strong appreciation looks excellent in most parts of the country.

GETTING STARTED

Should you buy or continue to rent? Of course, that's a private decision, but I hope you'll decide to buy. I've done both many times, and I can tell you I always feel better when I'm in a home I own (even if the payments hurt!).

In the following chapters, we'll look at what you need to know to get a home you'll love and be able to afford. We'll consider location, finding the "perfect house," getting a really good deal, arranging for low-cost financing, saving money on taxes, buying when you're a single person and a host of other important topics, such as how to negotiate with the seller and how to read and understand the paperwork. Remember, anyone can rush out and buy a house. The trick is getting the right house, at the right price, in the right neighborhood.

Dream Home or Doghouse?

CHAPTER 2

Do you have a home of your dreams?

Interestingly, most people with whom I've talked have only a partial idea of what they truly want in a home. For some, it may be a particular look: a colonial with shutters, or a plantation style with pillars in front, or a Tudor with those cute brown boards on white plaster, or a western-style ranch. Others simply want room to roam: lots of bedrooms, a big kitchen and a bigger family room on a large lot. Yet other first-time buyers are looking for good schools or a close-to-work location and aren't that concerned about the appearance of the house.

Do you know what you really want in a new home? My wife and I certainly didn't when we bought our first home. And we made some significant mistakes. She was pregnant with our first child and I was struggling with a new job. Of course, we liked the idea of having three bedrooms and couple of bathrooms with a garage instead of a carport. But we didn't really talk much about it, and the "home of our dreams" came down to something we could get into fast that didn't cost a lot of money. And that's what we bought—a home that we quickly came to dislike.

While the house itself was small but adequate, the neighborhood was horrible. There were marauding gangs, and neighbors across the street who would simply throw their garbage out onto their lawn. Needless to say, we didn't enjoy living there, and what was worse, we had a terrible time reselling the property. Potential buyers would take one look at the neighborhood, particularly the homeowners across the street, and not even bother to stop and look at our house.

After living there awhile, we discovered what we truly wanted in a home, and heading the list, for us, was a good neighborhood. We also wanted a bigger backyard and a separate family room. If only we had known this *before* we bought! (As it turned out, we did eventually sell and move into a much more suitable home.)

There's an old saying that you can't get what you want until you first know what it is. That certainly applies to homes. Therefore, before you call an agent or do anything else, it's important to sit down and create a list of your priorities.

HOW DO YOU CREATE A "WANTS" LIST?

How do you really know what you want in a home until, as we did, you buy one? One not very helpful thing to do is to create a "dream" list; that is, a list of everything you've ever dreamt of having in a home.

The trouble here, as you'll soon find out if you try it, is that this sort of a list isn't practical. If we let our imaginations run away, pretty soon we're coming up with huge master bedroom suites with fireplaces, saunas and spas, palatial grounds with tennis courts and pools, views of mountains, oceans or lakes, maybe even set in a lovely European countryside! In other words, most of our dreams are just that—wishful thinking not grounded in reality. But there's nothing more real than spending $100,000 or more on a home.

Therefore, I suggest a different approach. I've found that while most of us may not always know what we *do* want, we are pretty certain about what we *don't* want (as in my own case). If you've been living in a rental setting, there may be a variety of things you want to avoid when you buy your first home. So first I suggest you list the things you want to avoid. Once you get those down, you can easily convert them to a positive "wants" list. A typical first-time buyer may want to avoid small bedrooms; a noisy location; a carport or no open parking; lack of laundry facilities; a location that's dangerous, far from work or far from family and friends; no outdoor garden area; and no nearby recreational facilities.

Your list, of course, may be far different. But you get the idea. While it may be hard to realistically visualize what you would want in a home, it's not so hard to put down what you want to avoid. Create your own list and discuss it with your significant other or with friends. What do you really want to get away from by buying your first home? This, after all, gets to the heart of why you want to buy in the first place.

Once you develop a list of negatives, it's easy to change it to positives. Let's take our list and convert it.

Positives Converted from Negatives

Things to Avoid	*What You Really Want*
Small bedrooms	Large bedrooms
Noisy location	Quiet location
Carport or open parking	Garage
Off-site laundry facilities	On-site laundry facilities
Far from work	Close to work
No outdoor garden area	Yard or garden area
Far from family and friends	Close to family and friends
No close recreation area	Nearby recreation facilities
Dangerous area	Safe area

Notice how easy it is to first make a list of things you want to avoid and then to change them from negatives to positives. While

Figure 2.1   Create Your Own "Wants" List

Things to Avoid	What I Really Want
1. _____	_____
2. _____	_____
3. _____	_____
4. _____	_____
5. _____	_____
6. _____	_____
7. _____	_____
8. _____	_____
9. _____	_____
10. _____	_____

you may want to take some of the items from my list, you will probably also want to add several of your own. Take a few minutes to stop reading now and create your own "wants" list (see Figure 2.1).

HOW DO YOU PRIORITIZE YOUR "WANTS" LIST?

If you ask people what they want from a list of desirable things, and they're honest about it, they'll tell you, "I want them all!" Of course, we all do. However, in the real world, particularly given the high cost of housing, it may not be possible to get every item on your "wants" list. Therefore, it's helpful to prioritize—to come up with those things you want most and those that, if forced to, you can get along without. How do you prioritize a "wants" list?

When we prioritize, we're basically asking ourselves to weigh the relative value of different items. Which carry heavier weight with us and which lighter? The factor that carries the heaviest weight with me is location. Notice that on my list there are five elements that concern the location of a future home: quiet, close to work, close to friends and family, close to recreation, and safe.

While your list may differ in other respects, I doubt it's really much different in terms of the first priority—location. Chances are that several items on your list will be location-related. For example, you may have listed "close to schools" or "close to shopping." Real estate agents know that the single most important consideration for the vast majority of people who buy a home is where that house is located. (You'll recall in the example of my first house, the biggest mistake my wife and I made was not paying closer attention to the location of our home.)

I'm not trying to talk you into making location your first priority. You may, indeed, have some other first preference. However, I am suggesting that if you want your first home to be a successful purchase, you should think seriously about putting location very high up on your list.

Even within the heading of "location," there are priorities. Is safety most important? Or is it being close to relatives and friends? What if the two are mutually exclusive? Which one is more important? In other words, while location may head your list, you'll eventually have to pick a spot where you'll begin looking. So now is as good a time as any to come up with at least some tentative indications of where you want to locate.

After location, it's really a toss-up about what's most important to you. You should ask yourself about the current and future size of your family. Are you planning to have children? How many? If you're going to have many children, then you'll want to think about a house with more bedrooms. Ask yourself just how important a garage or basement is. If you work on cars or have hobbies, it may be vital. On the other hand, maybe you can give it up for the sake of more bedrooms. What you should do is come to a decision about what's more important and start prioritizing your own list.

BUY WITH AN EYE TOWARD RESELLING

I'll repeat it many times in this book: You make your profit on your home not when you sell, but when you buy. Buy right and you'll find it easy to resell. Buy wrong, and selling for a profit can be almost impossible. Buying right means, of course, getting a good location. But it also means buying a home that others will want to own. In terms of bedrooms, the most popular single-family home has three; a two-bedroom home is usually too small (a one-bedroom home, except in the case of a condo, is very difficult to resell) and four bedrooms often push the price too high.

You will move. Notice I'm not saying that you *might* move. Unless you're the very rare exception, you will resell the home you're now buying within seven to nine years of ownership and buy another. That's statistical fact compiled by U.S. Department of Commerce. So you might want to remember, when making your list of priorities, that it's not for all time. If you don't get some special thing you want in this house, there's a good chance you'll get it in the next.

HOW SPECIFIC SHOULD YOU GET?

I have seen first-time buyers who have a prioritized list of what they want in a house right down to the exposure (southern, northern and so on) of the home. Some even go so far as to come up with a drawing of the ideal layout the house should have.

My feeling is that while it's important to know what you want, it's just as important not to get bogged down in details before you even begin to look. Remaining flexible is the key to finding the right home. Try not to be too specific. If you get locked into a specific formula for a home, you may quickly become disappointed when you discover that either it simply isn't out there or, if it's out there, you can't afford it.

GETTING STARTED

This first priority list is only to give you direction. Now, armed with your list, you're ready to get started. Once you begin looking in earnest, you undoubtedly will modify your list several times.

One final word of advice, however: Don't change your first priority, whatever it is, no matter what. If you have to give up everything else, get your first priority. If you don't, you'll never be happy with your first home.

Finding a Productive Agent

CHAPTER 3

Most people never have reason to use an agent until they buy their first home. After all, agents are usually found in career fields like acting or writing. Unless you're an actor or a writer, why would you want an agent? The reason is that in real estate, agents handle the vast majority of homes that are for sale. Most sellers "list" with an agent. Thus, when you call an agent, he or she often has access to 90 percent or more of all homes currently for sale in your area. (We'll discuss that last 10 percent sold "by owner" at the end of this chapter.) It only makes sense to check with an agent first.

But do all agents have access to all homes? Does it matter which agent I select? How do I find a good agent? In this chapter, we'll answer these and many other questions regarding agents.

WHAT IS AN AGENT?

An agent is a "fiduciary." This simply means that agents must act for their client (you) and in their client's best interests. For example, instead of looking for a house for yourself, you can hire an agent to do it.

WHOM DOES AN AGENT WORK FOR?

Because an agent works for a client, it's important to understand who that client is. Even though an agent may take you around to see different properties, most often you are *not* the agent's client. Rather, the client is the seller—the person who signed a listing agreement with the agent. This is an important concept to grasp, because it can make a big difference when it comes time to negotiate a purchase.

If the agent signs a listing agreement with the seller, thus becoming a "seller's agent" (a technical term), that agreement normally binds the agent to procure a buyer (you) for the property. This has some interesting ramifications. For example, if the seller tells the agent "Although I'm asking $80,000 for the condo, I'm willing to take $60,000, but don't tell the buyers," that agent cannot ethically tell you what the seller said.

On the other hand, if you tell the seller's agent "I'm offering $60,000 for the condo, but I'd be willing to go as high as $70,000," that agent is duty-bound to reveal this to the seller. He or she is working for the seller, not for you.

If there were only one property to look at, this might be fairly evident. However, agents usually "co-broke" virtually all the properties in an area. That means that although only one agent listed it, he or she will split the commission with any agent who brings in a buyer. Usually the other agent now becomes a "seller's agent" as well. In other words, just because an agent didn't list the property you're being shown doesn't mean that he or she isn't representing the seller.

Because of confusion over representation, many states today require agents to tell you exactly who they represent before you make an offer. An agent has three choices:

1. Seller's agent—as we've explained above.

2. Buyer's agent—This agent works for you.

3. Mutual agent—This agent purports to work for both buyer and seller. (I say "purports" because I don't think anyone can honestly serve two masters.)

THE BUYER'S AGENT

A buyer's agent is a relatively new concept in real estate. This is a person *you* hire to find a property for you. The buyer's agent goes out and examines all the properties available and then, I would hope, shows you the one that's best suited to you. If you're like me, I'm sure you're already raising the issue of payment. Do you as a buyer have to pay this agent?

Yes and no. Some buyer's agents do want payment from the buyer, often partly in advance, and often a rather small amount when compared to a full selling commission. On the other hand, they may co-broke with other agents and, hence, will often split the seller's agent's commission, meaning you may not have to pay them anything.

At this point you might reasonably ask whether splitting the seller's agent's commission might not constitute a conflict of interest for the buyer's agent. Interestingly, it's been held that the fiduciary relationship isn't necessarily determined by who pays the agent, but rather by who the agent declares is the client. In other words, in theory, a buyer's agent can be loyal to you even though he or she gets paid by the seller.

Should You Work with a Buyer's Agent?

In some areas, buyer's agents are plentiful—or at least available. In other areas, you couldn't find one if you spent a month looking. For myself, I really don't care who the agent technically represents as long as he or she is forthright and honest. I just keep to myself what my best offer is and what I'm willing to negotiate. Trusting yourself before your agent has been and still is the very best policy.

WHO ARE AGENTS?

Real estate agents come from every walk of life. Frequently they are people retired from another job who are looking to supplement their income. Sometimes they are women who are seeking to return to the job force after having raised children. I once read a study of successful agents that claimed that those who did the best in real estate were former women's shoe salesmen!

Regardless of what an agent used to do, there are certain attributes that make for success in real estate. Among them are

- honesty;

- the ability to get along well with people;

- a knack for numbers;

- good character judgment; and

- the ability to think logically.

Note that number one is honesty. The last thing in the world you want is to work with an agent who has a hidden agenda or who is trying to trick you into doing something that may not be in your best interests. You want an agent who will tell you the truth, even when he or she knows that you may not want to hear it or that it may mean losing a sales commission.

HOW DOES SOMEONE BECOME AN AGENT?

To become a real estate agent today, a person must obtain a state license. This involves paying a fee and taking a test. In some states the test is quite extensive and covers most aspects of real estate, including listing, selling, financing and ethics. Also, a person who has been convicted of a felony cannot usually become an agent.

Real estate agents go by several names: broker, salesperson and REALTOR®. As a first-time buyer, you may never have worked with an agent before, and it can be confusing. In any event, it's important to know the differences so that you can better judge the person with whom you're dealing. The terms listed below may help you make those distinctions.

Agent—Anyone who is licensed to sell real estate.
Salesperson—The entry-level position in real estate. Usually, in order to become a salesperson, you must not only pass a test but also get a broker to sponsor you. Then you must work in the broker's office for a number of years until you gain sufficient experience to become a broker yourself.
Broker—A person who has experience and has passed a more extensive qualifying exam. Only a broker can open and maintain a real estate office. One broker, however, can work for another. If the person with whom you're dealing tells you he or she is a broker, you know you're talking with someone who is one level above a salesperson.
REALTOR®—A broker who is also a member of the National Association of REALTORS® (NAR), a trade organization. NAR offers seminars and programs that allow brokers to increase their knowledge in fields such as exchanging (trades), leasing (rentals) and business opportunities (commercial real estate). Usually a REALTOR® will quickly let you know if he or she has an additional designation earned by taking special training. At the state level, agents belong to organizations associated with NAR; at the local level, they join real estate boards.
REALTOR-ASSOCIATE®—A salesperson who is a member of NAR.

DOES ANYONE REGULATE AGENTS?

Regulation of agents is twofold. Official regulation comes from the state. An agent can be disciplined for breaking the law and for unethical conduct. Some states are quite strict in their regulations; others are more lax. However, keep in mind that in order to be disciplined, an agent must do something substantially wrong. Just because you don't like what an agent says or because you end up with a house that isn't what you wanted doesn't necessarily mean the agent did something wrong.

Whom Do I Turn to if I Have a Problem with an Agent?

Agents can be disciplined by their peers through a local real estate board. If you have a problem, sometimes appealing to a local real estate board can be your most effective and immediate means of getting a remedy. An appeal to the state will usually take longer, and while it could ultimately result in the censure or discipline of the agent, that's not likely to help you immediately with your current problem.

HOW DO I FIND A GOOD AGENT?

That, of course, is the big question. I've worked both professionally and as a principal (buyer) with hundreds of agents. Some I wouldn't want to be in the same room with; others I'd trust enough to give a signed blank check. The agent that you get can make an enormous difference in finding the right home for you. With a good agent, the search for a home will be pleasant, the negotiations will be handled with dignity and chances are you'll be very pleased with the house you finally buy. On the other hand, with a not-so-good agent, every step of the way can be difficult, resulting in a place you really don't want.

Open Houses

There are many different ways to find an agent. Just walk into any open house and you'll discover that the agent on duty there is trying to cultivate you as a client. In the lingo of the business, you're a "prospect." Generally, the purpose of holding open houses is primarily to find buyers for the agent and also to give the appearance of doing something for the seller. Studies have repeatedly shown that buyers who walk into an open house rarely buy that particular property. I myself, however, am an exception to the rule, having bought a home I saw at an open house.

Agent's Office

Another way to find an agent is to walk into any real estate office. Just like in an auto dealer's showroom, you'll immediately be introduced to an agent.

However, if you're a "walk-in," you normally get the person who is "next up," or next in line. Agents are assigned "floor duty," or time they spend in the office answering calls on ads and responding to prospects who drop in. In a larger office there's a list, and you get the next person on the list.

That's not necessarily a good thing for you, however. The newer agents are usually the ones who want floor time, as it helps them get clients (prospects). Often the more experienced, seasoned agents have enough referrals to keep them busy. That doesn't mean they don't want a new client; every client is a potential sale and commission. It's just that you're not likely to get that better agent by just walking in.

Recommendation

Yet another way to find an agent is through recommendations. Perhaps friends or relatives recently bought or sold a house and had a good experience. They're probably thrilled to tell you about their agent. Call that agent up and interview him or her. Get a list of properties the agent sold over the past six months and the names and phone numbers of the buyers or sellers he or she represented. Then call those people and see what they say. Are they satisfied as well? If so, you've probably got a winner.

Other Ways to Find an Agent

You can use the Yellow Pages, or call on an advertisement in the paper, or check the bulletin boards at grocery stores (or computer bulletin boards). You can also look for For Sale signs (which often list the selling agent), see whose name comes up most often and call that person. Of one thing you can be sure: You won't have trouble finding a real estate agent. Some sources estimate that 1 out of every 100 people has a real estate agent's license. While 1 percent might not seem so high, that's nearly three million agents nationwide.

TYPES OF AGENTS

It's usually unfair to type-cast people, even a group. But when it comes to real estate agents, I find it really is helpful, particularly to first-time buyers. So, here are four other agent categories that you should know about.

Listers.   These are agents who make their living primarily by listing property. They rarely sell the properties they list. They simply have learned how to get people to put their homes up for sale. You would probably not want this agent to work with you as a first-time buyer. If you're not sure about the agent you have, ask how many homes he or she listed over the past year. Then ask in how many sales he or she represented the buyer. That should give you the answer.

Sellers.   These agents make their living by selling properties that others have listed. They tend to be assertive and very knowledgeable. However, as a first-time homebuyer, you may not want to enlist their services, as they may be too aggressive for you. If a buyer doesn't purchase within two visits, "seller" agents tend to move on. Their strategy is either to focus on the buyer most ready to act or to convert a buyer to action. It's the latter I worry about, where the agent pressures the buyer to make an offer. As a first-time buyer, that's not something you need.

Part-time. These are people who have their real estate license but for one reason or another don't work full-time in the business. Often they are retired and see real estate as a way to supplement their income without a full commitment to the business. A significant portion of all real estate agents are part-timers. The problem is that a person who works part-time at anything never really gets very good at it. Would you want to be in an airplane that had a part-time pilot? Would you want to deal with a part-time banker? Why, then, would you want to risk one of the biggest purchases you'll ever make with a part-time agent?

Don't know if the agent is part-time? Ask how many hours a week he or she spends selling real estate. If the answer is anything less than 50, you may have a part-time agent. If they say they work mornings, or afternoons, or only on weekends, watch out. They're part-timers.

Full-time. Finally, there's the full-time agent. This is a person who both lists and sells; who attends all of the sales meetings and the local real estate board meetings (where new properties are brought up and discussed); who works mornings, afternoons, evenings and weekends; and who makes a living (probably a good one) at it. This is the person you want as your agent.

HOW DO YOU HELP YOUR AGENT GET WHAT YOU WANT?

Once you find an agent you're happy with, you want to help that agent as much as possible to get you just the house you want. You don't want to be like the sick person who walks into the doctor's office and, when the doctor asks what's wrong, says, "You're the doctor—you tell me!" The more help you can give your agent, the sooner you're likely to get the right home.

Begin by showing your agent your prioritized "wants" list. This should immediately help determine what you're looking for. If nothing else, it should narrow down the neighborhood. Then, by looking at a number of houses, you should be able to quickly determine what the market's like and narrow your selection of home types.

Don't hesitate to tell your agent what you want. Telling is one of the surest ways of getting. That also applies to price. Let your agent know how much you can afford to pay. (We'll see how to calculate that in Chapter 6.) It will help narrow your search enormously. But keep in mind that most agents won't want to trust your figures. They will want to calculate for themselves just how much you can afford—which brings up another point of major concern to many first-time buyers: How much should you reveal to your agent about your finances and purchase plans?

HOW MUCH SHOULD I TELL MY AGENT?

You need to tell your agent enough so that he or she can effectively help you get the house you want. That includes some basic financial information, such as your income, your expenses and any bad credit that could ruin your chances for getting good financing, as well as how much cash you have available for a down payment. No, you don't need to write out a list of this information and present it to the agent; but on a need-to-know basis, you shouldn't hold back. For example, you may be looking at property that will require a 20 percent down payment. If the property costs $100,000 and you have only $5,000 in the bank, you're not going to be able to buy the property. (Some properties require no down payment at all—check into Chapter 11.)

On the other hand, when you eventually do find a home, you are going to wonder just how much to offer. Should you offer close to asking price or make a "lowball" offer? Do you think you can get this property for a steal, or will you have to pay until it hurts? (For more help here, refer to Chapter 7.)

To some extent, the agent can act as a coach for you in these matters. But be sure you know who the agent is working for—and if it's the other party, don't reveal your bottom line. Further, unless you negotiate directly with the seller (something I don't recommend for a first-time buyer), the agent will have to try to get your price for you. Therefore, sometimes it helps if you can do a little innocent acting for the agent's benefit. For example, the seller wants $110,000 for the house and you're willing to offer $95,000. The agent looks at the offer and wrinkles up her nose. That's almost 15 percent below asking price—a tough offer to get accepted. So maybe the agent turns to you and asks, "You know that they'll probably reject this offer. If they do, will you be willing to come up another $5,000 or $7,000?"

Now, if she's a buyer's agent, and you agree, you can be fairly sure she won't tell the seller what your plans are. But how hard will she try to sell your offer of $95,000 when she knows you're willing to pay $102,000? I'd be willing to bet that if she gets any reduction at all, it will be to $102,000!

On the other hand, you might say, "I won't pay a dime more than $95,000. If they won't take that, I'll look elsewhere!" If you say it with conviction and appear to mean it, the agent now has a different set of cards to deal with. She may suspect you'll pay more, but then again maybe you won't. As a result, she knows that she had better get the seller to either accept your offer or come as close to it as possible. In short, she doesn't have the buffer zone that she would have had before.

All I'm suggesting here is that you properly prepare your agent for the negotiations.

CHANGING AGENTS

It's important to remember that your commitment to your agent is only as strong as the service that he or she gives you. If your agent makes a big effort to find properties to show you every weekend, keeps calling to let you know as new properties come on the market and is helpful in showing you homes you want to see, by all means continue working with him or her.

But if your agent neglects you, doesn't call and doesn't show you properties you like—in other words, doesn't service you—you shouldn't feel bad about trying out a new agent.

One word of caution, however: Be loyal to the agent with whom you're working. At least give that person a chance. It can get terribly confusing if you're out with one agent on Friday, another on Saturday and two more on Sunday morning and afternoon. What if two agents show you the same house? Regardless of who brings in the offer, the other may claim that he or she is entitled to at least a part of the commission for having first shown you the property. That gets a bit sticky. The last thing you want is to have the agents fighting among themselves instead of fighting for you.

Just as you feel loyalty to an agent with whom you work, he or she will develop a loyalty to you, and when it comes time to make offers and counteroffers, that could be an important consideration.

Certainly, if you don't like an agent, or if you feel neglected or not properly serviced, move on. But it's to your benefit to give each agent with whom you work at least a chance to show his mettle.

Selecting the Right Type of Home

CHAPTER

Some first-time buyers just know they want a single-family home, no matter what. They were brought up in a house, are renting one now, and that's all they'll settle for. (If you're in this group, however, you might be pleasantly surprised by some of the features of "shared" living, as we will discuss later in this chapter.)

Other first-time buyers are apartment dwellers and only know the shared lifestyle of living in proximity to other tenants. If you're in this latter group, you may not know whether you'd like a single-family detached home or if you might actually prefer to continue in some form of shared living.

WHAT TYPE OF HOME WILL YOU LIKE?

As soon as you begin looking for a home and working with an agent, you'll be asked if you want a single-family detached home (only one house on a lot, not attached physically to another home) or are willing to live in a condominium, townhouse or co-op. One of the reasons the agent will ask is because single-family homes are the most expensive. You may not be able to afford a single-family home in the neighborhood you want. To get into a particular neighborhood, you may have to opt for some sort of less expensive "shared living." Another reason is that you may prefer some form of shared living. To understand the considerations in different types of homes, let's examine each separately.

What Is a Single-Family Detached Home?

This is the traditional house (see Figure 4.1). It stands alone on its own lot with separate back, front and side yards. Usually it has a garage or at least a carport.

Figure 4.1   Single-Family Housing

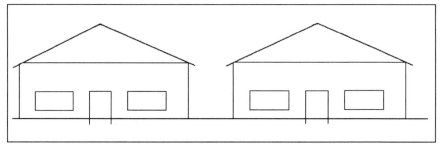

What Is a Condominium?

This is a legal term that means, in essence, that everything outside your home is held in common with other owners. A condo may be one unit of a 12-story building containing 120 units. Or it could be one unit of a four-unit building (see Figure 4.2). It's important to understand that what's described here is the legal means of ownership. You own separate title to your unit (at least the inside) and title-in-common with the other condo owners to the exterior walls, roofs, walkways, yards, and so on.

Figure 4.2   Condominiums. You own only the the "airspace" within your outside walls. You may have other condos below, above and to the sides.

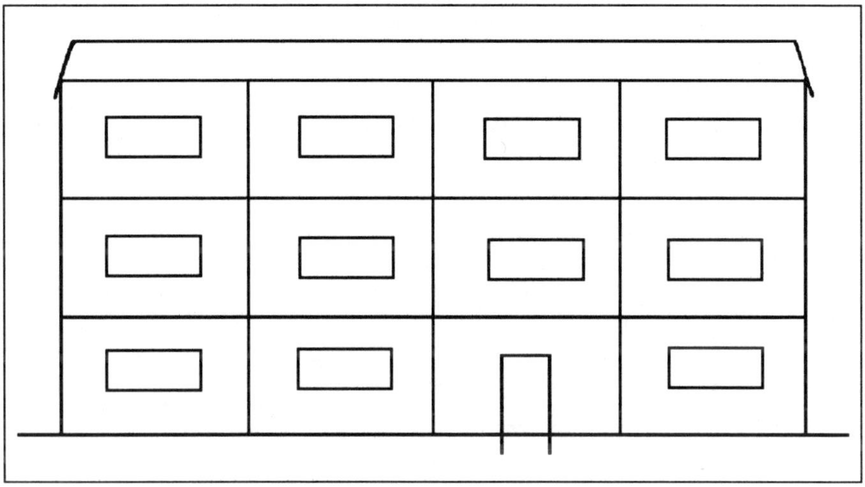

What Is a Co-op?

This is another legal term. It means that instead of owning title to your unit, you own stock in a cooperative that owns the entire property. However, the cooperative allows you to live in one unit because you are a shareholder. Under this structure, the co-op owns all the property including the common areas. You can sell your co-op by selling your stock. However, co-ops often have much stricter rules about who can buy and who can lease the units.

What Is a Townhouse?

This is a specific kind of a condominium known as a planned unit development, or PUD. In a PUD, there are no units above or below you, although you may share common walls with other units (see Figure 4.3). As a townhouse owner, you own the land under your unit and the air above, although all the walkways and common areas are still shared. This is important, because a PUD or townhouse development typically will have a much lower density than a condominium development. The noise and congestion, consequently, are usually much greater in a condo and less in a PUD. Hence, PUDs or townhouses are more desirable and usually cost more.

Figure 4.3 Townhouses. You own the ground beneath and the air above, but you share common walls and grounds with other owners.

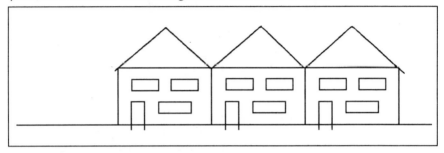

WHY WOULD YOU WANT TO "SHARE" A HOME?

There are several reasons why first-time buyers in particular will find a condo, townhouse or co-op attractive. The first, which we've already seen, is price. In any given area, a shared home of roughly the same size is going to cost less than a single-family home. (The exceptions are metropolitan areas such as Manhattan, where there is a premium for good co-ops.)

Another reason is that you don't have to be bothered with exterior maintenance. As with an apartment, there's no yard work (although townhomes will often have a small yard area where you can plant a lawn or garden). Further, you don't have to worry about your neighbors taking care of their property. From the outside, at least, the homeowners' association (HOA) will maintain the upkeep of the entire development. It is, in fact, this lack of maintenance and the similarity to apartment living that entices many first-time buyers.

Yet another plus is the amenities. A good shared property will offer recreational facilities that sometimes include pools, spa, tennis and/or racquetball courts, bike trails, weight training rooms and perhaps the option to rent a large central room for parties. This offers all sorts of recreational possibilities, including the opportunity to meet new friends. In a well-developed property, your individual unit will be relatively isolated to maintain your privacy, yet the overall property will have many amenities available should you choose to use them.

WHY YOU WOULD NOT WANT A "SHARED" HOME

On the other hand, there are several drawbacks. Historically, the prices of shared homes (with certain exceptions, such as the co-ops in New York City) have always been lower than those of single-family detached homes. Part of the reason is that it costs less to build a condo or co-op, and the units themselves take up less space on valuable land.

However, a point not often mentioned by those selling shared homes is that they simply have not appreciated as well as single-family homes. In a recession, condos typically are the first to lose buyer interest. And in an economic expansion, they are the last to be sold. In short, over the last 20 to 30 years, shared homes have generally been considered less desirable than single-family homes and, as a result, have commanded lower price appreciation and seen slower resales.

One reason for this is that investors have always bought up significant portions of new condo developments and then rented out their units. As a result, in some developments up to 50 percent of the units are rentals. Because tenants don't have any real stake in the property, they tend not to take as good care of the units as owners do. And this tends to lower overall property values in the development.

However, during the last recession, when real estate prices plummeted in nearly all parts of the country, there was a big fallout of investors, many of whom had mortgaged their condos to the hilt in anticipation of reselling quickly for a big profit. Many lost their condo units to foreclosure, while others simply sold at rock-bottom prices. As a result, at many developments today the proportion of tenants to owners has changed significantly. Fewer tenants and more owners have once again made these properties more desirable.

Another minus for condos when compared to single-family homes is the density. As in an apartment building, you have a lot of bodies living relatively close together. Noise can be a problem. Finding parking can sometimes be a headache. And there's a condominium homeowners' association (HOA) that always seems to impose countless rules about conduct, which sometimes can be a real burden on the owner.

Yet another potential problem is that if one of the other condo owners gets angry at the condo association, he or she can sue. If the lawsuit is successful, you can be docked for the costs. I belong to a condominium HOA that recently lost $100,000 to an owner's lawsuit over where a commercial vehicle could be parked. The HOA was responsible for that loss, meaning it had to be shared among the 350 of us who were members. Fortunately, an insurance policy picked up the costs, but that's not always the case.

Finally, in a shared home, you never achieve the sense of "my home is my castle" that you get from a single-family detached house. You can't go outside and bang on the wall or put up a swing or paint your front door (on the outside) without permission (which often is not forthcoming) from the HOA. Many people find these sorts of restrictions so stifling that they refuse to live in shared homes.

WHAT RESELLS BEST?

As I noted earlier, taking resale potential into consideration at the time you buy is very important if you want to turn a profit on your home. While in Chapter 2, we talked about what you may want in a home; now I suggest that you also consider resale value. In other words, what are the features that most buyers look for?

The fact is that certain features in a home can make it more or less resalable later on. Remember, if you buy the wrong kind of home now, that could be a problem down the road.

While the public's taste in homes changes, listed below are several features to look for that will make a big difference when it comes time to resell.

Most Desired Features in a Home

House Size. There was a time when the only rule regarding the size of a home was "the bigger, the better!" However, as modern families have gotten smaller and the price of large homes has increased, this is no longer the case. While a small home is still hard to resell, today a very large home is also difficult. A middle-size home, usually between 1,500 and 2,000 square feet, will resell faster in most neighborhoods.

There are, of course, exceptions. In metropolitan areas where costs are astronomical, a small, 800-square-foot co-op might resell instantly, while a 2,000-square-foot unit, much more expensive, might languish on the market. On the other hand, in some very expensive areas, a 3,500-square-foot home might go right away (because that's what people expect when they pay over $500,000 for a house), while a small, 1,800-square-foot home might sit for months with no offers. In short, go for a medium-size home unless you're in a market that demands a different size.

By the way, an agent can almost always tell you the square footage of a house. And after you look for a while, you'll be able to gauge it pretty well yourself.

Lot Size. This really only applies to a single-family home. Some people want a large lot with "room to roam." The problem with a large lot, however, is upkeep. You will have grass to mow, shrubs to trim and leaves to rake, plus a bigger watering bill. So, while some people may like a large lot, most people do not. It is, in fact, more difficult to sell a house with a very large lot than one with an ordinary size lot.

What's large and what's ordinary? A great deal depends on what's usual for the neighborhood. However, a typical suburban lot is between 5,000 and 10,000 square feet. Anything over 10,000 square feet (roughly a quarter-acre) is considered overly large (except in very expensive neighborhoods).

Bedrooms and Baths.   The rule here is not too few and not too many. If you can avoid it, never buy a home with only one bathroom. Two bathrooms, even if one is only a "half-bath" (no tub or shower), are considered a necessity by most people. After all, what do you do if two people need to use the bathroom at the same time and there's only one?

More than two bathrooms is nice but not necessary, and it often only adds to cost. In very expensive homes, of course, the number of bathrooms is sometimes simply a measure of status.

The ideal number of bedrooms is three, although in a shared-living arrangement, two bedrooms often will have to do. It works like this: There's a master bedroom (with its obligatory bathroom), a child's bedroom and a second child's bedroom or guest room. If you don't have children, of course, it may not matter to you. But when it comes time to resell, chances are it will matter to the buyer. Most parents like to put each child in his or her own bedroom, or, if there are more than two, to separate the boys from the girls. That's why three bedrooms works out well.

Four bedrooms is nice for bigger families. But often builders will put four bedrooms in the same number of square feet as three, which means you end up with smaller rooms all around.

Room Size.   Big rooms are always better. Particularly look for a large master bedroom, large family room, good-size eating area off the kitchen, and a kitchen large enough to work in. Although huge bathrooms—particularly master bathrooms—have become fashionable, I don't believe the size of the master bath is that critical a selling feature. Neither is the size of the other bedrooms and the dining room, although buyers will notice if they are particularly small. Because most people spend most of their time at home in the family room, it's usually more important than the living room, although a larger living room "shows" the house better.

Modern Features.   Often what separates a "fixer-upper" from a polished home in the minds of buyers are the fixtures in the kitchen and bath. Modern, good-looking fixtures including basins, faucets, ovens and countertops are a must. If you purchase a home without modern features, plan on putting them in yourself before it's time to resell. Not only will you get all of your money back (assuming you do a good job) in an increased price, but the home will sell much faster.

Design.   The design of the home needs to fit the neighborhood. If every house is a ranch style and yours is a southern plantation style, it will stick out like a sore thumb. Try to find a home that complements the neighborhood rather than fights it.

Condition.   This is a big area that we'll cover in Chapter 9 on home inspections. However, the condition of the property is going to be critical to your ability to resell. A worn-out roof will either kill a sale or cost you money (lots of it) to repair or replace. Old carpeting, dirty ceilings and walls, battered doors—all of these are important to buyers. That's why it's sometimes much easier to buy a newer property (under ten years old) than an older one. There's simply less wrong with it; it's in better condition.

There are, of course, other important features, such as the way traffic flows through the home, how nice the entrance looks and the "curb appeal," or how appealing the house is when potential buyers first drive up.

A good rule of thumb to remember is that what strikes you as very nice about the house will probably appeal in the same way to most other buyers. Similarly, what you find undesirable, others will probably find undesirable, too.

This translates into "you get what you pay for." Lower-priced properties often have problems. You may be willing to accept the problem in order to pay a lower price. However, that same problem (unless you can somehow correct it) will earn you a lower price later on when you resell.

Choosing the Best Location

CHAPTER 5

In one sense, finding the right location is easy. Because everyone wants it, it stands to reason that the best location is going to be the most expensive one. So simply look for the most expensive neighborhood in town and you're there!

As we'll see in the next chapter, however, many of us simply can't afford the "best" neighborhood. So instead of wishing for what we can't have, let's take a look at what we really can get in a neighborhood.

CAN AN AGENT HELP?

Looking for your first home can be tough enough without duplicating work that others have already done. (You don't want to reinvent the wheel, so to speak.) Therefore, I suggest you think about working with an agent at the onset. (Check back to Chapter 3 if you're not sure about how to find a good one.) The agent, presumably, has already spent years learning all of the different neighborhoods in the community you are considering. All you need to do is to tell this agent a few important facts and figures about your income, cash available and credit, and he or she should quickly be able to determine (roughly) the top price you can pay for a home. (Don't just take the agent's word for it; figure it out for yourself, as seen in the next chapter.) Then you can be shown all the neighborhoods that fit the bill.

Note: You can usually assume you'll be able to pay about 5 percent more in price than the agent figures (or you figure after reading the next chapter) you can afford. The reason is that you probably won't pay full price, but instead will get a seller to come down around 5 percent. But remember, this is just a rule of thumb, so don't expect it to work perfectly every time. Some sellers won't budge in price!

HOW SAFE A NEIGHBORHOOD DO YOU WANT?

If you're working with an agent and he or she is honest, one of the questions you will be asked concerns safety. How big a priority is a safe neighborhood for you?

If you're from a rural or country area, this question may seem strange. But if you're a city dweller, it's going to be right up there near number one in terms of priority.

There are many ways to measure the safety of a community. Probably the most accurate gauge is the number of crimes committed each year. This information is available from a variety of sources, including the U.S. Department of Commerce and some chambers of commerce (usually only those communities with the safest records make them readily available to the public). This statistic is also usually broken down in terms of armed robberies, homicides, burglaries and so on.

Real estate agents who deal with homes in various neighborhoods day in and day out often can simply tell you off the top of their head which are the safest. However, agents are particularly wary of recommending or discrediting any neighborhood when their words could be interpreted as being racially biased. Hence, when you ask, you have to be specific: You want to know which neighborhoods have the lowest crime rates, not which neighborhoods are "far from the ghetto or slum."

Today, it can be argued, there are no truly safe neighborhoods. Crime seems to occur everywhere. Some neighborhoods, though, are safer than others, and a good agent should be able to quickly point this out to you. However, safety has a price. Generally the safer neighborhoods are also the more expensive ones.

WHAT ABOUT SUBURBAN DECAY?

We've all heard of urban decay. That's when inner-city buildings and neighborhoods get old and the nicest people move away, leaving those that either can't afford to move or are not so nice. But most people are unaware that the same thing is happening in the suburbs.

Most of America's suburbs were built, or at least started, right after World War II. The period 1946 through 1965 saw an enormous surge in homebuilding as people moved away from the decaying cities and into the "safer, cleaner and cheaper" suburbs.

The trouble is that the builders typically built homes with a 30- to 40-year horizon. That means that homes built in the late '40s, '50s and early '60s are now decaying and falling apart themselves. Further, these early suburban homes were often small (around 1,200 to 1,500 square feet) by today's standards and did not have many of the features (two full baths) that most people want today.

As a result, the early suburbs are now in a state of decay. From Los Angeles to Minneapolis to Boston, many cities are experiencing suburban crime and social decay formerly found only in the inner city. Unfortunately, these are also the more affordable, close-in areas.

As a result, first-time homebuyers are cautioned about simply looking to the suburbs as a panacea. Many are as ridden with crime and social problems as the inner cities used to be. Indeed, some inner cities are now experiencing a rebirth that makes them more desirable than the "'burbs!"

In short, don't be narrow-minded about what you'll consider in terms of location, and don't simply point yourself toward the suburbs. You could be making the mistake of buying yesterday's good areas.

SHOULD SCHOOLS BE AN IMPORTANT CONSIDERATION?

There are two perspectives when it comes to schools, and they tend to be determined by whether people have school-age children or not. Those who have children understand the importance of good schools and are willing to move to neighborhoods in which the schools excel. Those who don't have school-age children often couldn't care less about the schools and are happy in neighborhoods where the schools are dismal. This is fortunate for the latter group only because homes in those neighborhoods with bad schools are usually much cheaper.

Actually, in my opinion (shared by some others), the single most important ingredient in determining long-term housing values in a neighborhood is the quality of its schools. Time and again I have watched neighborhoods start out similar in every way, except for their schools. Those in which the residents passed bonds to help their schools saw property values jump. On the other hand, those in which schools deteriorated because school bonds seldom or never passed tended to see property values increase only slowly, or in some cases actually decline. The biggest difference was not the size of the homes or the overall location of the residential neighborhood, but the quality of the schools.

If you have children or are planning to have them, then this should be a big consideration. However, even if you aren't planning to have children, you should also consider it if getting more for your house when you sell is important. Remember, if you're willing to accept lesser-quality school districts, an agent can immediately show you lower-priced neighborhoods, ones in which you'll more easily be able to afford to buy. But you'll pay the piper when it comes time to sell and you find that your home hasn't gone up very much in value.

By the way, while having good schools is important, it's also nice to be located fairly near the school so your children can walk. Being close to a bus pick-up is the next best thing. Beware, however, of locating directly across from the school. You'll have noise and crowds of kids on your front lawn every season except summer.

HOW IMPORTANT IS SHOPPING?

A lot depends on whether or not you have a car. If you're a city dweller who depends on public transportation, then having a grocery store, pharmacy or hardware store nearby can be crucial. Because you'll probably be carrying everything you buy (or at least wheeling it), having stores close by is an important consideration.

However, if you live in the suburbs and have a car, then having shopping close by is far less important. In California, for example, first-time as well as experienced homebuyers rarely, if ever, ask about shopping. They just assume that they'll have to drive about 20 minutes or more to get to it. (It's very rare that shopping is going to be more than 20 minutes away from any neighborhood. But it's a good idea to ask, just in case.)

If convenient shopping is important to you, be sure to stress that fact to your agent so you have a better chance of getting what you want.

DO YOU WANT PUBLIC TRANSPORTATION NEARBY?

Once again, urban readers are going to find this an important consideration. If you plan to live in or near Boston, for example, you will probably want to be sure you're close to an MTA station. Otherwise, getting into and out of the city could be a problem because of congested streets and limited parking.

On the other hand, if you're living in Phoenix, you'll want to know that you're close to one of the freeways. If not, you'll spend a great deal of time on surface streets trying to get from one side of the city to the other. If it's a commute, it could be tough. In the San Francisco Bay area some commuters have a two-hour drive in from Stockton each day. They want to be sure they're not going to have to add another 15 minutes getting to and from the on/off ramp.

A friend of mine recently moved to Palos Verdes, a desirable community on the water near Los Angeles. However, he had to commute to Ventura, a driving distance on freeways of about one and a quarter hours during off-peak times. (Distances for commuting today are given in time rather than mileage; it's more accurate, given the traffic situation in most areas.) However, he didn't realize that access to freeways was poor in Palos Verdes. He had to drive on surface streets for 20 to 25 minutes before getting to a freeway, adding substantially to his commute. If he'd have thought about it earlier, he might have chosen to live closer to his work.

WHAT ABOUT LIVING CLOSE TO RELATIVES OR FRIENDS?

It's important to remember that while buying your first home is not a forever proposition (remember, most people move every seven to nine years), it is a long-term one. On the other hand, relationships with people—even relatives—tend to wax and wane. While right now you may be on the best of terms with your relatives and love to go out with your friends, what's going to happen if you buy close to them and the relationship sours? What happens if in a year or two you suddenly don't want to see them anymore—but they live right across the street from you?

I'm suggesting that you reconsider if you've made this a high priority. Instead, be more interested in getting good schools and a safe neighborhood. You can always drive an extra 20 minutes to see Aunt Hildy or brother Jack or Ted and Louise.

WHAT LOCATION SHOULD YOU LOOK FOR WITHIN A NEIGHBORHOOD?

Let's say you've listed your priorities, you've gone out with an agent and you've found the perfect neighborhood. It's relatively safe, not too expensive, close to freeway access and public transportation—in short, it's just right. Now, is there anything special to consider with regard to the houses in that neighborhood?

Yes, there certainly is. In a later chapter we'll consider the house itself, but for now, let's discuss its specific location. Certain home locations within neighborhoods are considered more desirable, while there are others you will want to avoid.

Corner Lot. As a first-time buyer, you may have heard that a corner lot is more desirable, because it's usually bigger than the surrounding lots. True, it is bigger. But it is *less*, not *more*, desirable for two reasons. First, a corner lot has two front yards (one facing each street), and a smaller backyard (the house "wraps" around the lot, leaving less room in back). This means that you'll have to spend more time in your "public" front yard mowing the grass and trimming the hedges, and you'll have less room to enjoy yourself privately in your smaller backyard. In short, a corner house offers more work with less reward. Further, a corner lot has traffic going back and forth on not just one, but two streets. That means more noise, more congestion and, to a small extent, less safety.

Therefore, most people prefer *not* to have a corner lot. You won't enjoy it as much while you're there, and you'll have more trouble selling it.

Key Lot. A key lot is one that butts up to a corner lot on one side in some tracts (see Figure 5.1). What this means is that while other lots will have two side yards and the backyard of only one other lot will abut them, a key lot will have only one side yard and two backyards will abut it.

Some people aren't even aware of a key lot, while others avoid it. The only real problem comes when it's time to sell. Then, chances are you'll get less for your key lot than other standard lots.

Figure 5.1   Key Lot. The back and at least one side face the backs of other lots.

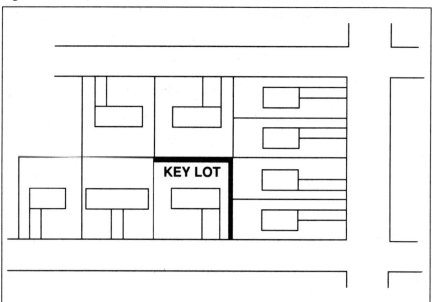

Flag Lot.   A flag lot looks like a pole with a flag on the top (see Figure 5.2). The pole is the driveway and the flag is the lot. The lot is surrounded on all sides, except for the driveway, by the backs of other lots. Usually it came into existence because there was an irregular-shaped block that left an empty area in the center after all of the lots were divided. The builder, rather than make this a common park area, decided to eke a few more dollars of profit out of it: He installed a driveway between two standard lots for access and sold it.

Flag lots normally sell for less (because they are much less desirable) and, when it comes time to resell, are extremely difficult to dispose of. Don't be tempted by their low price. You could spend years trying to resell, at an equally low price.

Green Belts.   Some communities are built with common areas around homes. These are green belts that often contain walkways and bike paths. A green belt should be considered a valuable asset and will almost certainly add to the price of the home. It will also

Figure 5.2 Flag Lot. Landlocked with access only through a narrow driveway.

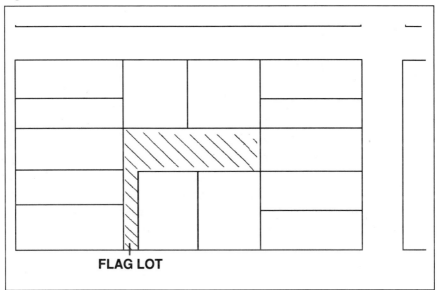

make the home easier to resell later on, and you'll get a better price for it. If you have the option, look for a neighborhood that has green belts.

Anchor. Many neighborhoods have an "anchor," and that can be good or bad. For example, one type of anchor is a community center with a swimming pool and spa available to all the local homeowners through a homeowners' association. The anchor is considered a plus and helps boost the price of the property at resale time. It also makes selling far easier.

On the other hand, some neighborhoods have anchors that drag them down. For example, a neighborhood that butts up to an industrial site is a drawback. If that site produces noxious fumes, it's a double drawback. If that site happens to be a toxic dump, you can probably forget about ever reselling the property. (So don't be charmed by its amazingly low price!)

Try to determine what the anchor is for the neighborhood you are considering. Then, ask yourself if the anchor boosts the location or drags it down. If it's enough of a drag, you may want to avoid buying there.

Lot versus House.   Another important consideration is the relationship between the area the house occupies and the size of the lot. If you have a big house on a small lot (as is commonly the case where land is very expensive), your yard maintenance will be minimal. On the other hand, if you have a very large lot with an average-sized house on it (as is often the case in the country), you will have a lot of maintenance. Extensive maintenance is costly (when you have to hire a gardener) or takes a lot of time and effort if you handle it yourself. With a large lot with gardens or lawns in back and front, plan on spending at least one morning every weekend on maintenance to keep it up properly. That can be a very sobering thought for someone who's lived the last few years in an apartment and had the weekends totally free of maintenance work.

WHAT SHOULD YOU LOOK FOR IN A CONDO LOCATION?

In terms of the overall location of the development, the same rules hold as for a single-family home (as described above). However, there are some additional considerations with regard to your unit's location within the development.

High or Low?   Some people, particularly women who live alone, prefer to live on the top floor of a two- or three-story building or on the upper floors of a taller building. Usually this is a safety consideration, as it's unlikely you'd find a burglar climbing into windows at that level.

However, living on a top floor is also important because of noise. There's simply less noise upstairs than downstairs. If people below you jump on the floor, you won't hear it. But if those above you jump on the floor, you'll know it instantly!

Low-Sound Location.   In addition to upper floors, some locations are quieter than others. These include locations away from the street or parking lot, from washing machine areas, and away from the pool or open-air recreation area; units that are on a corner of the building (rather than sandwiched between two other units); and units that are isolated from other units by having a garage or open area between them.

The question, of course, is how do you know how quiet a particular condo unit is? Unfortunately, you don't until you live there—or until you try it out. Before buying, I strongly urge you to visit the condo at various times, such as at seven in the morning, at dinnertime and later in the evening, at least once on a weekday and once on the weekend. That will give you a pretty good idea of what the noise conditions are like.

By the way, don't worry that the owners will be inconvenienced by your coming by. If they want to sell, they'll just have to put up with it. (So will you, when it comes time for you to sell!)

View Unit.   Many condo developments will have some units that face the parking lots, while others face a view such as a mountain or lake. If you have a choice, take the better view. You'll enjoy it while you live there. And you'll sell quicker and for more money later on.

SHOULD YOU BUY DIRECTLY FROM A BUILDER?

Thus far we've been assuming that a real estate agent takes you around to see a variety of neighborhoods in your price range and that fit your priority list. But suppose you discover that there's a neighborhood with new homes in which you'd really like to live. Should you deal directly with the builder?

The answer here has to be both yes and no. Keep in mind that builders tend to be rather inflexible about financing and price. If you deal with them, you'll have to do your negotiating face-to-face. If you deal with their salesperson, he or she will often not have your interests at heart. In short, you could end up spending more money than you want to by choosing a new housing location.

On the other hand, new homes in good areas generally tend to appreciate faster than older homes in the same area. The reason is simple: Everyone wants a newer house. It's more desirable, so while it may cost more initially, it probably will not only go up in price faster but will also resell sooner.

One alternative is to use a real estate agent to negotiate with a builder. Often builders, particularly in a slow market, are willing to pay a real estate agent's commission for buyers. Look at the homes yourself, but then have the agent make the offer.

CAUTION: If you "sign in" when you first look at a new home (many builders have a sign-in sheet as you walk through the front door), you may be excluding yourself from the opportunity of having an agent represent you. By signing in, you give notice that the builder brought you in, not the agent, and the builder could refuse to pay a commission to the agent (depending on the listing agreement), even if the agent presents your offer. Remember, there's no requirement that you sign in when you look at new homes.

Beware of Unfinished Homes in Unfinished Developments

Spec builders—those who build without having presold the property—want to find buyers as soon as possible. Thus, they will often begin selling as soon as the property is subdivided, sometimes even before streets and utilities are put in. They may, for example, ask for only a small deposit—say, $250—to hold a lot. Or they may want $2,500 to hold a half-finished building.

There's nothing wrong with putting up your money in advance of the development or house being finished, as long as it *gets* finished. Too often, however, I've seen developers build more dreams than homes. The properties don't sell as fast as anticipated and the builder runs out of money. Construction stops, with many homes half finished. If that happens, you may have to spend many months arguing with lawyers to get your money back.

Similarly, until the development, tract, full condominium or whatever is complete, you won't really know what it's going to look like.

Parks and common areas shown on drawings may end up being far less attractive when actually built. What's worse, if the builder runs out of money, half the tract (in which you're living) could be finished, while the other half could be a wasteland of framed walls, rough plumbing and dirty streets for months or even years. It won't be a pleasant place to live, and it could be an impossible home to resell.

Look for completed homes. You may have to wait, and it may cost a bit more, but you could save a fortune in headaches.

Affording Your Palace

CHAPTER 6

The trouble is that while most people (including many who live there!) cannot afford a Beverly Hills location, most of us want to live there. Therefore, finding a home is often a compromise between what we want and what we can afford.

In the past two chapters, we went into detail on the type of house most people may want and where they want it to be located. In this chapter we're going to get a dose of reality. We're going to find out what we can afford.

Keep in mind that the reason there is so often a discrepancy between what's affordable and what's desirable (besides the champagne taste/beer budget syndrome) is that real estate is so expensive. It's the high cost of housing that often forces us to compromise on our wishes in order to satisfy our pocketbooks.

However, the home of your dreams may be closer to reality than you realize. As a matter of fact, it usually turns out that most people can afford a lot more house than they think.

JOINING THE MORTGAGE RANKS

I'm going to assume that you're not one of the lucky few who can pay cash for their home. (Statistically, less than 10 percent of all home sales are actually for cash.) That means you're going to have to borrow most of the money you will use to buy your first home. You're going to join the ranks of the 60+ million Americans who have monthly mortgage payments.

The real question now becomes how big a mortgage you can afford. And it all comes down to the monthly payment. The bigger the monthly payment, the larger the mortgage, and the larger the mortgage, the more expensive the house you can afford.

There are two ways to determine how big a mortgage you can afford, both valid. The first limiting factor is the size of a mortgage that the bank will give you. The second is the size of the mortgage payment that you feel you can handle. Let's take the latter first.

How Big a Mortgage Payment Can You Handle?

When asked how big a house payment they feel they could handle, most first-time buyers usually think of how much they are paying in rent and use that as a basis. For example, if you're paying $500 a month in rent, you may figure that you can afford to pay $500 a month on a home that you own. The problem is that rental payment doesn't necessarily translate directly into mortgage payment.

The reason is that when you buy a home, you will be paying more each month than just the principal and interest on your mortgage. You will also have taxes, homeowners' insurance (of course, as a tenant, you may also have been paying renter's insurance), maintenance and repairs, possibly a homeowner's fee and other costs.

On the other side of the coin, you will have some tax write-offs that aren't available to tenants. The interest on your mortgage (which is almost all of the payment) and your taxes are deductible (up to maximum amounts for interest). That means that some of what you pay on your mortgage and property taxes you'll save on your income taxes.

Because of these extra costs plus extra savings, most first-time buyers are quite a ways off when figuring what they will be comfortable with in terms of a mortgage payment. To determine your comfort level, you need to perform the following four calculations:

1. Determine the biggest housing payment you feel you can handle.

2. Calculate your extra monthly costs.

3. Figure your tax savings.

4. Add those savings to your estimated maximum house payment.

1. Determine the Biggest Housing Payment You Feel You Can Handle. Start by calculating your total current expenditures each month and see how much is left over for a total house payment. See Figure 6.1 for a budget to help you calculate your current expenses. Try to be candid. Put down what it actually costs, not what you wish it cost!

Now subtract this total from your take-home income, and that's how much you should have left that can be applied toward the house itself.

Monthly Income versus Expenses

$_____ **Total monthly income**

Less $_____ **Total monthly expenses**

= $_____ **Total Left for Housing**

If what's left isn't very much, ask yourself what you might be willing to give up.

Remember, there's the appreciation and the value of home ownership to consider. You may be willing to strain and pay more for a home of your own than you would for a rental. Further, you're buying a home, not renting, and when you sell, you'll (we hope!) be making a profit. Think of this as an investment, not money simply

Figure 6.1 Total Expenses *Without* Rent

$_____	Food
$_____	Utilities
$_____	Telephone
$_____	Auto/health insurance
$_____	Medical payments, pharmaceuticals
$_____	Car payments
$_____	Gas, oil, other car maintenance/repairs
$_____	Public transportation
$_____	Alimony
$_____	Child support
$_____	Kids' costs (clothing, school expenses and so on)
$_____	Child care
$_____	Eating out
$_____	Clothing
$_____	Entertainment
$_____	Big-ticket purchases (furniture, computers, etc.)
$_____	Vacations
$_____	Hobbies (videotapes, CDs, books, magazines, etc.)
$_____	Clubs
$_____	Other
$_____	Add 5 percent for extras overlooked
$_____	TOTAL MONTHLY EXPENSES

thrown away. On the other hand, don't go overboard and create a payment that will sink you.

Strain, but don't fantasize!

2. Calculate Your "Extra" Costs. Don't make the mistake of thinking that all you'll need to pay will be your mortgage payment. As noted earlier, there are other costs involved in maintaining ownership of a home. The list below will help you calculate them.

Extra Monthly Costs

$_____ **Yard maintenance and landscaping**

$_____ **Home repair (Buying a newer house helps here.)**

$_____ **All utilities—gas, electric, water, garbage, sewage, phone, cable (Some of these are paid by landlords when you rent.)**

$_____ **Homeowners' association dues (if any)**

In addition, there will be property taxes and fire/homeowners' insurance to pay. You probably won't have a handle on these figures until you have a specific house in mind. For now, take 10 percent off the total monthly amount you figure you have for housing expenses.

You do the math:

Estimating Taxes and Insurance

$_____ **The amount you have available for housing expenses as shown above**

$_____ **X 10% for taxes and insurance**

$_____ **Total Extra Home Costs**

Now add your "extras" plus taxes and insurance and subtract from the amount you have available for housing. That will give you the amount you have left over for a mortgage payment.

Estimating Amount Left for Mortgage Payment

My Figures		Your Figures
$1,300	Maximum comfortable payment	$_____
$ 300	Less "extras" and taxes and insurance	$_____
$1,000	Left for Mortgage Payment	$_____

3. Figure Your Income Tax Savings. Remember, you can deduct your taxes and most of your mortgage interest from your income taxes. You've already calculated your property taxes above. Now, determine your interest on the mortgage. While the actual calculation is quite complex (because almost all of the monthly payment for the first five years of a standard 30-year mortgage goes to interest), as a rule of thumb, you can deduct virtually your entire mortgage payment. That's what we'll do here.

Now, what is your marginal tax rate? Tax rates vary according to your income. At the bottom of the scale, some people pay at a 15 percent rate. Others who have a very high income pay at a maximum 39 percent rate. I'm going to assume that your top marginal tax rate is 28 percent. (Check with your accountant or tax preparer if you're not sure; it's an important figure that you should know.)

Calculating Monthly Write-off

My Figures		Your Figures
$1,150	(including interest and taxes)	$_____
X 28%	(marginal tax rate)	X 28%
$ 322	(Monthly Tax Savings)	$_____

This means that because you can now deduct mortgage interest and property taxes from your federal income taxes, you'll save money—in my example, approximately $322 a month. (Remember, the actual figure will be slightly lower, because not all of the mortgage payment is interest; some is principal. It will be significantly higher if you're in a state that has high state income taxes, because you can deduct mortgage interest and taxes here, as well.)

4. Add Your Write-off to the Amount You Can Afford for a Mortgage. This is the step that confuses many people. But it's simple to understand *if* you remember that first you must calculate your tax savings, then add those tax savings back onto your mortgage payment. Don't do it the other way around. Don't add your tax savings to your mortgage payment, then calculate your write-off. That would be like counting the same dollars twice.

Mortgage Payment You Can Afford After Tax Considerations

My Figures	*Your Figures*
$1,000 **(left for mortgage payment)**	**$**_____
+ $322 **(monthly tax savings)**	**$**_____
$1,322 **(Adjusted Monthly Available)**	**$**_____

How big a mortgage can you get for $1,322 (or whatever your figure came out to)? The answer depends on other variables, such as the term (length), interest rate and type of mortgage, such as adjustable or fixed rate. See Figure 6.2 for examples at different interest rates.

Note the amazing difference in mortgage amount as the interest rate increases. The higher the interest rate, the lower the maximum mortgage you may qualify for. This is why it is important to purchase, if at all possible, when interest rates are low.

Also keep in mind that what we've just calculated is the payment with which you will feel comfortable. If you're the sort of person

Figure 6.2 Maximum Mortgage Amounts at Different Interest Rates

Mortgage payment of $1,322 for a 30-year fixed mortgage				
7%	$200,000		10%	$151,000
8%	$182,000		11%	$139,000
9%	$164,000		12%	$128,000
Mortgage payment of $1,322 for a 15-year fixed mortgage				
7%	$147,000		10%	$123,000
8%	$138,000		11%	$117,000
9%	$130,000		12%	$110,000

Mortgage payment of $1,322 for an adjustable-rate mortgage with a start rate of 5.5 percent

5.5% $235,000

who's pretty good at keeping track of your checkbook and at budgeting, chances are this is a fairly accurate figure. If, on the other hand, your checkbook tends to be off each month and you never can stick to a budget, then perhaps you'd best pay close attention to the next section.

HOW DO LENDERS CALCULATE YOUR MAXIMUM PAYMENT AND MORTGAGE?

Even though you may figure that you can afford a maximum monthly payment and mortgage amount as shown above, there's no guarantee that a lender, such as a bank or savings and loan, will agree. They could calculate that you can only afford less—or more! Therefore, it's important to understand how lenders calculate mortgages to get an idea of what you probably can qualify for.

One way to do this is to check with a lender. This is a good idea in any event, because once you buy your home (or perhaps even before, if you "prequalify" for a mortgage), you will have to go to a lender to get a mortgage. A lender can quickly ascertain how big a mortgage and mortgage payment you will qualify for just by asking you a few questions and making a couple of calculations.

How Do You Find a Lender?

You can locate a lender simply by looking in the Yellow Pages of your phone book under the following headings:

- Mortgages

- Mortgage Brokers

- Banks

- Savings and Loans

If you belong to a credit union, you can check there, also.

I suggest that you call a couple of lenders, at least one being a mortgage broker. Banks, savings and loans, and credit unions will each have different mortgage programs that they will be happy to explain. (See Chapter 11 for information on the types of mortgage available to you.) However, a mortgage broker usually represents dozens—sometimes hundreds—of different lenders, some out of state. Thus, a single mortgage broker can often provide you with enormous variety. (Chapter 10 goes into more detail on the differences among types of lenders.)

Why Should You Make the Lender's Calculations Yourself?

The problem with allowing a lender to determine the maximum mortgage payment and amount you can qualify for is that you won't know if the lender is doing it right or not. Further, if you go to three lenders, you might get three different calculations, which can be very confusing. (A lot depends on the program the lender is pushing at the time you call.) The only way to be really sure is to know how to do it yourself.

By the way, in the parlance of real estate, what we're talking about here is "qualifying." We're asking how big a mortgage and mortgage payment you qualify for.

How Do Lenders Determine How Big a Mortgage To Give You?

Lenders qualify homebuyers on the basis of three factors:

1. Creditworthiness

2. Income

3. Amount of down payment

Let's consider each separately.

Creditworthiness

This simply means how assured the lender is that you will, in fact, repay the mortgage. After all, you could buy your home and then never make a payment. The lender would have the hassle of foreclosing, taking the property, perhaps fixing it up and then reselling. Quite frankly, lenders want to make money only by earning interest. They are not excited by the prospect of owning and reselling property. (In fact, it makes them look bad, because it means they made a bad loan.)

Therefore, at some point in the homebuying process, you will be asked to submit to a credit report. As if that isn't enough, you'll also be asked to pay for it (usually only around $35)!

Note: Some first-time homebuyers will contact a lender *before* they find their home and ask to be qualified. Many lenders will do this

and then issue a letter saying that "Mary and John Smith have qualified for a mortgage of up to $...." This can then be handed to a
prospective seller, and I guarantee it will enhance your chances of
getting a sale. Given a choice between two buyers who are offering
roughly the same deal, a seller will choose the prequalified buyer
every time.

Credit Reports.   You should be aware that there are two types of
credit reports used. There's a simple credit report that a lender may
request when you first apply for a mortgage. It usually seeks out
your credit only in the area in which you live. However, before the
mortgage is actually funded, the lender will always also request a
"three-agency" credit report. This is a combined report from the
nation's three largest credit reporting companies, TransUnion, Equifax
and TRW. All of which means that if you have any bad credit, it will
be caught.

And that's a problem. Lenders like perfect credit—no blemishes,
no late payments, no defaults and, God forbid, no foreclosures. If
you have perfect credit, and a lot of it (it's important that you have
borrowed and paid back many times in order to establish a credit
track record), a lender will offer you the best interest rate and mortgage available.

On the other hand, if your credit is slightly blemished (a late payment here and there, a dispute and perhaps a corrected default a few
years ago somewhere else), you may still get a mortgage for the
amount you want, but it could be for a higher interest rate.

Or, if you have a serious credit problem, such as a bankruptcy or
(the worst for mortgage lenders) a foreclosure, you could be denied a
mortgage.

Sufficient Income

Besides demonstrating a track record of paying back loans to prove
your creditworthiness, you must also show that you earn enough
income to afford the monthly payments. I've seen some people show
up at a lender's office with a prepared budget to explain just how
they plan to afford the mortgage.

This might work in the case of some very high mortgages (above $203,400), where the lender actually funds and then keeps the mortgage itself. But today most lenders only fund real estate loans, they don't hold them. Instead, they sell them to other lenders, including quasi-government agencies such as Freddie Mac and Ginnie Mae. These secondary lenders buy our mortgages from the lenders with whom we deal, collecting a little less interest than we pay. The difference goes to our lenders as profit. And our lenders often "service" the mortgage, or collect the payments, for an additional fee. (We'll have much more to say about this in chapters 10 and 11.)

To be able to sell your mortgage in this secondary market, the lender must meet the secondary lender's requirements, which are quite specific in terms of how much income the borrower (you) must have. These "underwriter rules" are usually quite strict, and your lender really has no choice. You can point to your budget to prove that you can afford a higher mortgage, but if you don't meet the underwriter's criteria, you simply won't get it.

So what are the underwriter's criteria in terms of income?

It depends on when you apply and on the particular underwriter. It also depends on how much cash you're putting down. However, as a general rule, the following underwriter guidelines apply in most cases of loans under $203,400 (as of this writing; the amount changes frequently).

If you put 20 percent down: Your total monthly payment, including mortgage, taxes, insurance and homeowner's fees (if any), cannot exceed 32 percent of your total monthly income before taxes, provided you have no other long-term debt. (Long-term debt means such things as car payments, alimony, credit card payments and so on that run for more than four to six months.)

If you put 10 percent or less down: Your total monthly payment, including mortgage, taxes, insurance and homeowner's fees (if any), cannot exceed 28 percent of your total monthly income before taxes, provided you have no other long-term debt.

Keep in mind that the above rules are general. At any given time, the underwriters can be slightly more lenient or more strict.

PERFORMING THE LENDER'S CALCULATIONS

Making the calculations for your income is really quite simple, but it does require that you be perfectly candid. (In most cases, the lender will require you to bring in proof of your income.)

First, figure your total monthly income. This means the amount that you earn *before* payroll deductions for taxes, insurance, retirement and so on—your gross income.

Next, subtract long-term debt, which includes any monthly payments for alimony and/or child support, as well as car payments, credit card payments and other loans running more than six months.

Now take either 32 percent (if you're putting 20 percent down) or 28 percent (if you're putting 10 percent down) of the resulting figure and that's the maximum monthly payment the lender will allow you to make. Here's a sample calculation.

My Figures		*Your Figures*	
$2,500	Gross monthly income	$_____	
-$ 275	Monthly long-term debt	$_____	
$2,225	Net Monthly Income	$_____	
X 28%	X 33%	X 28%	X 33%
$630	$734	$____	$____

CAN YOU GET AROUND THE LENDER'S MAXIMUMS?

What we've seen above is how it's done according to the rulebook. I've also mentioned that the rules are fairly strict because of the underwriter's requirements.

Sometimes, however, the rules can be changed or bent. For example, instead of using 28 percent or 32 percent of income, lenders will sometimes allow an increase to 30 percent and 34 percent (or may require a decrease to 25 and 30 percent), depending on the health of the economy and other market conditions. Ask the lender if the rules can be stretched.

Another possibility is to forget the underwriting rules described above and instead ask to be qualified in terms of your overall income-to-debt ratio. This is another tool that underwriters use, and it compares your total debt to your total income. (While you might think that the figures would come out the same either way, surprisingly they sometimes differ, often to the borrower's advantage.)

For this calculation to work, however, you must know in advance what your mortgage, insurance, tax and HOA (if any) payment will be. In other words, you can try this only if you already have a property in mind.

If you do, add up the total payment described above, then add in your long-term debt as explained earlier. Now calculate this as a percentage of your total income. If it's 39–40 percent, you could get the mortgage. Here's the calculation:

My Figures		*Your Figures*
$700	Mortgage, insurance, tax, HOA payment	$_____
+125	Long-term debt	$_____
$825	Total of Monthly Payments	$_____
$1,800	Gross income	$_____
$700/1,800	Payments as a % of income	$____/____
39%	Less than 40% usually gets the mortgage	____%

Yet another method is to put more cash down. If you can put, for example, 25 percent down, all the above rules go out the window. With that large a down payment, many lenders are thrilled to make you a loan without selling it on the secondary market and without an underwriter, and they can be extremely lenient when it comes to qualifying income.

How Much Can You Afford To Put Down?

As you may have noticed, many of our calculations have been dependent on how much money you can afford to put down on a property. Unfortunately, this is a sore spot for many first-time borrowers. After all, your entire down payment must come from savings. You don't have another house that you can sell and roll over the equity. This raises a series of questions.

Should I wait until I have saved up a large down payment before buying? Probably not. In most markets, the longer you wait, the more expensive the houses get. Also, if interest rates are rising, you want to get into the market as soon as possible. Besides, there is financing available that can get you in with as little as 5 percent down (that's only $5,000 on a $100,000 home) plus closing costs.

Can I borrow the down payment? Unfortunately, lenders do not allow you to make the down payment with borrowed money. However, if you borrowed the money a long time ago—say, three months or longer—it usually isn't considered borrowed specifically to make a home purchase, and you might get away with it.

Can I use a gift as a down payment? Frequently parents, grandparents or other relatives will gift money to first-time homebuyers to help with the down payment. (Generally, up to $10,000 annually of such a gift is nontaxable.) The trouble is that lenders like to get the names of the donors on the mortgage. For example, if your parents are giving you $10,000 to help with the down payment, the lender may require them to qualify and sign on as well as you. To get around this ridiculous requirement, just get the gift into your account several months before you apply for the mortgage. Then, if asked where you got the money, you can say it was a gift, but it won't look like a gift that was given specifically to help you buy a home.

Should I put down as much as I can or hold some money back? Remember, you need cash for more than just the down payment. There are also the closing costs. And you may want to buy some new furniture and, if possible, keep a reserve in case of emergencies. This would argue for holding back as much as possible.

On the other hand, the bigger your down payment, the smaller your mortgage and monthly payments. However, keep in mind that putting down an extra percent or two won't make that big a difference in monthly payments. Besides, most people feel that coming up with cash is the hardest thing to do, financially speaking.

How quickly must I come up with the down payment? Generally speaking, you won't need the full down payment until the transaction closes (usually when you move in). It could be a month or two or even more between the time your offer is accepted by the seller and the deal closes. However, you'll need to show the lender that you have the money to put down by referring to a savings or similar demand deposit account. And you'll need to have the deposit immediately. Your deposit check is usually cashed the minute the seller accepts your offer.

Should I put down more, if I can afford it? Few people are in this lucky position. Most of us strain to get the minimum down payment.

However, if you have the option of putting more down, should you do it? A lot depends on what your goals are. Putting more money down will reduce the amount of your mortgage, and that, in turn, will also reduce your monthly payments.

But unless you put a lot of extra money into the property, your monthly payments won't be reduced by much. On the other hand, you won't have that cash available in case you need it for other purposes. (You could, however, obtain a home equity loan [second mortgage] to get that money out, if needed. But then you'd be paying interest *on* it instead of receiving interest *for* it.)

Another way of looking at it is in terms of interest. As of this writing, if you have an extra $10,000 and put it in the bank, you'll be lucky to get 5 percent. On the other hand, if you put it into the house, you'll be avoiding paying an 8 or 9 percent mortgage on that amount of money. In other words, you'll save 4 or 5 percent.

Should you do it? It's really a matter of how you view money. I've done it both ways at different times of my life. When I was a first-time buyer, however, I hung onto the cash.

WHAT YOU THINK VERSUS
WHAT THE LENDER THINKS

In this chapter, we've looked at the maximum mortgage payment from two perspectives: the borrower's and the lender's. Of course, the lender rules. But be aware that just because a lender says it's so doesn't make it so. You may be able to handle a far greater mortgage payment than the lender says you can. Or you may be able to handle far less.

My suggestion is that you take whatever a lender says with a big grain of salt. Don't get the biggest mortgage available to you if you feel you can't handle the payment. On the other hand, don't settle for a smaller mortgage than you know you can handle, just because a lender says you can't; fight for it.

Understanding a Real Estate Transaction

CHAPTER 7

Because you're a first-time buyer (or haven't purchased for quite a while), you may be completely unfamiliar with the procedure for a property transaction. It isn't, after all, quite like going to the store and buying a bottle of ketchup.

We've already seen, in chapters 4 and 5, how to pick the ideal house and the right neighborhood. And in Chapter 3 we discussed getting a good agent to work for you. Now, let's walk through the purchase of a home to see what's involved. By the way, even though you may know many of these procedures, others may be unfamiliar. It's a good idea to stay with us in order to get the whole picture.

IN THE BEGINNING...

You already know much of the beginning. You make the decision to buy; you find an agent to show you around; you look for a house and a neighborhood. This process can take anywhere from a few days to many months, depending on what's available, how much you can afford and how choosy you are. (By the way, there's nothing wrong with being choosy. It just means you won't be satisfied until you get the right property.)

In many respects, the beginning is the most important part of buying, certainly for the first-timer. It's a time of investigation and discovery. Often you really won't know what you want until you've been looking for quite some time.

Therefore, I encourage you to take as much time as you need. It's probably better that you miss a "steal" (a below-market-priced home) than that you get something with which you'll be unhappy.

IN THE MIDDLE...

The middle is when you formally make your offer to purchase, the seller ultimately accepts and all the paperwork starts. For the first-time homebuyer, this part can be the most traumatic. I can recall a young man in his mid-thirties commenting on the experience who said something like this:

"I was asked to sign this piece of paper and then another. I gave them a check, then signed more papers and initialed others. They kept telling me what it was all for, but I couldn't make heads or tails out of it. I just signed and initialed and eventually I got the house!"

I'm sure the experience is similar for many others. So let's take it slowly and try to make sense of the different pieces of the puzzle.

Do You Need an Attorney?

And if so, at what stage?

The safe answer is that for a first-time buyer, yes, you do need an attorney, although in some states an attorney is seldom if ever used. You need an attorney as soon as you're asked to sign the first document, which is the offer. The reason is that the whole process, particularly the documentation, is new to you. Without competent legal advice, you won't know what's to your advantage and what's not.

How do you know you're not "signing your life away" with that offer?

Having said that, my own experience in the real world is that attorneys tend to muck up real estate deals. This is not a condemnation of attorneys, but rather a statement that when they do what they're supposed to do—namely, protect their clients—they tend to go so far overboard that the other party, the seller, is loath to accept the deal.

What you really need is someone who is legally competent to steer you to safe waters, but who also knows how real estate deals are put together and can come up with something the other side will feel comfortable signing. Out west, there are many good agents who fill the bill. On the East Coast, there has arisen a whole class of real estate attorneys who can handle this for you.

Yes, you want legal advice, but you don't want legalese. You want to be protected, but not to the point where no seller will touch your offer.

The Offer

When you find a house that you like, you have to give the seller some sort of formal notice that you would like to buy it. This is called the offer.

The reason it's called the offer is that most of the time people don't agree to pay what the seller's asking. As I noted at the beginning, it's not like walking into a grocery store: You don't (or most people don't) pay full price.

The reason is twofold. On the one hand, we all want to see how good a deal we can get. Maybe we can get the seller to come down a little bit. Or maybe we just can't afford to pay what the seller's asking.

How Much Should You Offer?   On the other hand, sellers frequently price their homes a little high, expecting a lower offer. Thus, they are prepared to come down, at least a small amount. You may get them to come down a large amount, of course, depending on how well you negotiate.

Statistically, most buyers initially offer at least 5 percent less than the asking price for the home. This does not mean they get that much off. The seller may counteroffer (we'll discuss this shortly). But as a general rule, it's a place to start. In a depressed market, you would, of course, probably offer less. In a hot market, you may want to offer close to full price.

If you have a good agent, he or she should be able to help you determine what is a reasonably good offer. Don't forget that the agent may represent the seller. But if the agent represents you, you could get some excellent advice. (Reread Chapter 3 if you're not sure about this.)

One excellent way to help determine not only how much you should offer but also how much the home is worth is to have your agent print out a list of comparable sales. Because almost all agents today are linked by computer, this should only take a few minutes. You'll be able to see what similar homes in the neighborhood sold for going back at least six months. You should also get a list of how similar homes are currently priced on the market.

Very quickly you'll be able to get a good idea of what a realistic price is. You'll also know if you are offering a good price to the sellers or a bad one, from their perspective.

The topic of negotiating the offer is a subject worthy of a book all by itself. It just so happens there is one: *Tips and Traps for Negotiating a Better Real Estate Deal*, by yours truly (McGraw-Hill, 1995). You may want to check it out before making your first offer.

The Deposit

It is customary, although not required, that a deposit (also called earnest money deposit) accompany your offer. The amount is up to you, but it should show that you are in earnest about buying the property. Keep in mind that it is possible that if the seller accepts your offer and you don't go through with the deal, you could lose your deposit!

At this writing, I suggest around $2,500 for homes under $100,000. You'll want to increase that by $1,000 or more for homes up to $200,000. Above that a maximum of $5,000 should be sufficient. By the way, it's a good idea to make the deposit check out to an escrow company rather than the seller. If you make it out to the seller (or his or her agent), you could have more trouble getting your money back if the deal doesn't go through.

The Counteroffer

The seller just might accept what you offer. It's happened before. If that's the case, then you've got a deal.

On the other hand, it's more likely the seller will "counter." That means that he or she has rejected your offer and is now making an offer to you. Keep in mind that the original offer and the counteroffer are separate. The seller can't both accept and counter; it's either one or the other. You're under no obligation to accept any counteroffer.

Typically, sellers will submit a counteroffer at below their asking price (although they may insist on the asking price and counter on the terms). Now the ball is back in your court. For many first-time buyers, this is a time of soul searching and hand wringing. Usually the counteroffer is better (for you) than the original asking price, but not as good as you offered. Should you accept it? Or should you reject it?

Again, your agent may be able to give you good advice. Just keep in mind, however, that you can't both accept the counteroffer and change it. Either you accept it exactly as it is written or you reject it. On the other hand, if you reject it, you can counter the counteroffer.

There's no limit to the number of counteroffers that can go back and forth. It's important to realize, however, that every time you counter, it means you've rejected the seller's last offer. The seller is under no obligation to continue with the game. He or she can simply pick up the marbles and go home, leaving you without a house. For that reason, I suggest you make your counteroffers as reasonable as possible.

The Sales Agreement

The document on which your offer (and usually on which the counteroffer) is made is called the sales agreement. Until both you and the seller sign, it's simply an offer. Once both parties sign, however, it becomes a binding agreement. For that reason, you should read it over carefully *before* you sign it, and have your attorney check it as well.

Note: Many people read only the parts of an agreement that are filled out at the time. The preprinted material (called "boilerplate") is often overlooked based on the assumption that it contains standard items necessary to all agreements. That's not true with a real estate sales agreement. Today, virtually all of the important information is in preprinted form. Very little is actually hand-written in. Read the boilerplate carefully. Have your agent and an attorney carefully explain anything you aren't sure about. For example, does the sales agreement specify that all wall and floor coverings are to be included? If not, the seller may be planning to take the drapes and carpets!

Sales agreements usually include at least the following components:

- Price and terms

- Time

- Contingencies

- Title

- Occupancy

- Walk-through

Price and Terms.   Be sure these are filled in accurately and that they reflect your understanding. The seller might accept your offer and you'd be bound to what was written in. If you put it down wrong, it's too late to back out; you'll have to live with it. Be sure you understand the terms. If you don't, have someone competent explain them to you.

Time.   Pay special attention to any time limits. You or the seller or both will have to live up to them if the agreement is fully signed.

Usually you will give the seller a set period of time to accept the offer. The shorter the time, the better. You don't want someone else to come in with a better offer while the seller is considering yours.

There's also the time it takes to complete the transaction. Be sure you allow yourself enough time to get a mortgage. Three weeks is an absolute bare minimum. Six weeks is more comfortable. Check with a mortgage lender first to find out how long it's taking to get financing in your area.

Contingencies.   Also, be sure that there are necessary contingency clauses. These are often included for your protection. For example, a typical contingency will say that the deal is "subject to" your obtaining appropriate financing. Or the sale is "contingent upon" your approval of a home inspection. This means that if you can't get the financing or don't like what the home inspection reveals, you don't have to go through with the deal. If these clauses aren't properly included, you might find yourself bound to go through with the deal even if there's no lender or the house is sliding down a cliff! If you fail to go through with the deal without contingencies, you might lose your deposit or, worse, get sued by the seller. Be sure your attorney checks these very carefully.

One important contingency to consider including is a home warranty plan. This guarantees that if there's a problem with any of the home's systems after you move in (a broken water heater, for example, or a gas leak or even a leaky water pipe), the warranty company will fix it. All you'll be responsible for is a small deductible. You won't have to hassle the seller or the agent about why they should have to pay and you shouldn't. Best of all, the seller normally pays for the warranty plan!

Unless it's specifically mentioned as a condition of sale, however, it won't be included and the seller won't pay for it. It's an important contingency you won't want left out.

Title.   Also check the way you'll take title. If you're married, you may be able to take title as either "joint tenant" or as "tenancy by entirety" or "community property." There's also individual tenancy and tenancy in common.

I am purposely not describing each of these forms of tenancy here, because what they are is not nearly as important as their financial and tax consequences. (I encourage you not to decide what to fill in by simply reading a brief description in other books.) There are very different tax and credit outcomes for each, and if you're not experienced in tax and law matters, you should not make the decision about how to take title without expert help. Indeed, in some cases how you take title can be the most important part of the entire sales agreement. Consult with a tax attorney or at least a tax accountant before declaring here.

Occupancy. The agreement should specify when you get to move in. Usually this is only after the deed has been recorded in your name. But it should be immediately after; otherwise, the sellers might not move out right away and you could have trouble getting them out. (At that point, they could be considered tenants and might need to be evicted, if they didn't want to freely move out.)

Walk-through. One last point: Be sure the agreement allows you a final walk-through inspection just before the sale is concluded. That way you can check to be sure the property is in the same condition it was in when you first saw it and the seller hasn't done anything to degrade it. This can be very important with a sloppy seller. Include it as a contingency.

THE END GAME

After the sales agreement is finalized, the seller signs, and all the "i"s are dotted and "t"s crossed, you have a deal. But you don't yet have a home. It's a long way between signing the sales agreement and getting the key.

During the next few weeks, both you and seller will have a lot of work to do to be sure that the sale is consummated. And normally, there is a time limit. One of the clauses in that sales agreement will usually say that you have only so many weeks to come up with financing and remove all contingencies in order to complete the purchase—typically four to eight weeks. No mortgage, no house.

The Mortgage

Your first chore is to obtain financing. Refer to the chapters on affordability (6) and financing (10 and 11) for things to do. Most important, you want to be sure that you have found an appropriate lender and submitted all the documents necessary to get a home loan. These will usually include the following items:

- Recent paycheck stub

- Two years of income tax forms (if you're self-employed)

- Credit check (ordered by lender, paid for by you)

- Verification of deposit (from a bank showing you have the necessary down payment on account)

- Verification of employment (from your employer showing how long you've been employed and stating your chances for continued employment)

- Appraisal of property (ordered by lender, but paid for by you)

- Proof of insurance on the property (you must obtain from an insurance company)

- Any other documents the lender may need, such as proof that you've paid off an old loan that shows up in a credit report as unpaid

You will also be asked to sign that you received a notice of mortgage costs statement. It must be given to you within three days. Read it carefully. You will have to pay for everything that's listed on it.

I suggest that you visit your lender of choice immediately to get the ball rolling and then call the lender every week or as often as necessary. Always ask if there's enough time for the lender to fund the loan. The lender should be saying yes. If the lender says no, it's an emergency situation. The mortgage is off track. Call the agent and your attorney, and if necessary, find another lender to get it back on track.

Escrow Documents

The escrow holder, whether it be an attorney or an escrow company, will ask you to sign escrow instructions. These reiterate everything on the sales agreement and instruct the escrow to gather all the documents, signatures and money necessary to close the deal.

This is usually a long form. Be sure you and your attorney read it carefully. Be sure it accurately reflects what was in the sales agreement. Once you and the seller sign it, it is as binding, if not more so, than the sales agreement. If there is anything different, point it out and have it corrected. Don't sign until it's right.

The escrow may also ask for a variety of other documents, including the following:

❏ *Identification sheet.* This will ask you everything about yourself, including previous addresses, other names used, former spouses and so on. It's necessary to identify you for recording title.

❏ *Payment vouchers.* Your sales agreement may specify that certain items are to be paid out of escrow at the time the deal closes. These may include such items as the termite inspection fee, home inspection fee, document preparation fee and so on. The escrow officer may ask you to sign each as a separate voucher or one voucher for all.

❏ *Title report.* The escrow will usually receive a preliminary title report on the property. This details the title and proves that the seller is indeed the owner and has the right to convey title to you. Your signature usually signifies that you've received a copy.

❏ *Agreement to pay for title insurance.* You want title insurance. This guarantees that your title to the property is good. In most areas, buyers pay for title insurance. In some parts of the country, however, sellers traditionally pay or the fees are split. You'll be told what's common for your area.

❑ *Homeowner's documents.* If you're buying a condo or co-op, you'll receive bylaws and other documents of the association. You should also receive a current financial statement as well as a report on any legal problems (such as lawsuits) faced by the association.

❑ *Other documents.* Anything that might be necessary to close your deal.

The whole process will take a number of weeks. However, when everything is completed, all documents are in, the loan is ready to fund and the seller has signed (or is prepared to sign) the deed, you'll be asked to come in to sign your final papers and turn in the money necessary to close the deal.

The Walk-through

If your sales agreement provided for it (and it should have), you'll be given the opportunity to reinspect the property before the closing (usually a day before).

Accompanied by the agent(s) and perhaps even the anxious seller, you'll see that the seller has moved out (or is completing the move out) and be shown that everything is as you first saw it. (Be careful of accepting a property with the seller still living in it. If the seller isn't out by now, when will he or she be out? You could end up with a seller as a tenant! Not a good idea.)

Now is the time to complain if something is amiss. But it's not time to try to back out of the sale unless something is very seriously amiss.

Look for recent damage and for missing items, such as wall or floor coverings, that were to be included in the sale. Has the yard been kept up? If not, perhaps the seller should pay for a gardener to get it back in shape. Make your feelings known if there is a problem. This is your last opportunity to check out the property.

SIGNING THE FINAL PAPERS

Once again, this can be somewhat frantic, with paper after paper put in front of you and check after check being written by you. Don't panic—but be prepared.

You're a first-time buyer (or a buyer who hasn't purchased in a long time). You don't know what you should sign and what you shouldn't. You don't have time to read each clause in every document. So what should you do?

Don't go to the closing by yourself. Take your agent along or, even better, your attorney. You want someone who's experienced, knowledgeable and competent to check every document along with you. You want to be sure the figures are right and that you don't pay too much. (Normally, the escrow will ask for a few dollars more than necessary in case of any unexpected expenses. If there are no additional expenses, this will be sent back to you later.)

If you go alone and don't know what you're doing, it can be frightening and expensive—much more so than the cost of having an attorney present.

Don't assume that all the documents are prepared correctly; they may not be. Don't assume that the escrow officer is on your side; he just wants to get this deal signed and done with so he can get on to the next. Don't assume that the sellers have done everything they were supposed to; they may not have.

The closing is your last chance to correct any mistakes. But as a first-time buyer, you probably won't know a mistake if it's as big as a fist sitting in front of you. So don't try to bull it through. Spend a few bucks to take someone along who knows the ropes. (Most real estate attorneys will include this in their overall fees for handling the sale.)

Note: Often agents do not want to accompany you to a closing because they are afraid that if anything is wrong later on, you will blame them. That's not good enough. They should be there to assist you, or they should have counsel there in their place.

The following need to be checked at the closing:

- *All documents*—to be sure the correct ones are there and that they are filled out correctly

- *The mortgage papers*—to be sure they are accurate

- *The math*—to be sure it all adds up. In my own experience, more often than not there's at least one math error at the closing.

IS IT OVER YET?

Yogi Berra's famous quip "It ain't over till it's over!" applies here. You go to the closing, sign everything until you feel as though you've had all the blood sucked out of you, and you still don't own the property!

The home isn't yours until the deed from the seller to you is officially recorded. This is done either first thing in the morning or the last thing at night at the county hall of records by the title insuring company. This is to ensure that a sneaky seller doesn't first dash down there and sell the property a second time to someone else. It's highly unlikely, but when lots of money and insurance are involved, all the precautions must be taken.

Before the deed can be recorded, however, your cashier's check has to clear and the lender has to fund the mortgage. The mortgage money is in the form of a lender's check delivered to the title insurance company for your mortgage amount. To avoid any potential problems, the escrow usually will not close until at least 24 hours after all monies have been deposited. At that time, the escrow will declare itself complete or "perfect," and the deed can be recorded.

Only after the deed is recorded will you normally be given possession of the property. (In special cases, possession can be given earlier by arrangement between buyer and seller, but that's most unusual.) Typically, the agent will meet you at the house, which by now has been fully cleared out, and present you with the key.

At last, the home is yours. Now you can begin thinking about reselling!

For a detailed explanation of the pitfalls to avoid and how to get a better deal when buying, I suggest my book, *Tips and Traps When Buying a Home* (McGraw-Hill, 1990).

Saving on a
Fixer-Upper

CHAPTER 8

The real trouble with real estate, as any first-time buyer will attest, is that it's too expensive. Everyone remembers how low-priced real estate was just a few years ago. But for most first-time buyers, the train has already left the station—and even with the big real estate recession of the late eighties and early nineties, prices still seem very high today.

As a result, many first-time buyers who are finding that the neighborhood they want is just a bit out of their reach are looking for alternatives. And a fixer-upper frequently comes to mind as the first, best alternative.

A fixer-upper is a needy house. For one reason or another, it's been neglected to the point where its condition has lowered its market price. While surrounding well-maintained homes, for example, may be selling for $150,000, the fixer-upper may be priced at $135,000 or less. The only reason for this is that it's a mess. The seller wants out and realizes the only way to accomplish that is to take less money.

Many first-time buyers see this as a real opportunity. The lower price may get them into a neighborhood they might not otherwise be able to afford. However, not all fixer-uppers are opportunities; some are money pits. In this chapter we're going to look first at whether you should really consider a fixer, and then we'll see how to find one that you can handle.

OPPORTUNITY OR MONEY PIT?

The big advantage that fixer-uppers have, which is perfectly obvious to everyone, is that they are cheaper. What many buyers fail to appreciate, however, is that they are cheaper for a reason: their poor condition. What this means is that after you buy one, you have to fix it up.

I can hear many readers saying, "That's okay with me. I love to putter and fix things. I'd be a natural at fixing up a home."

Maybe. But when you buy a true fixer-upper, a house with a price substantially reduced because of severe problems, you're going to have to come up with a lot of extras.

EXTRAS NECESSARY FOR HANDLING A FIXER-UPPER

Money.   The first extra is money. Not only will you need the money to buy your first home, but you'll also need the cash to fix it up. How are you going to get it if you're strapped for funds?

There are several options. Sometimes you can put less cash down and get a bigger mortgage, leaving you with the wherewithal to fix up the property. Sometimes you can get a home equity loan from a lender, almost as soon as you purchase your home. (I got one within 30 days of a purchase.) This can also help finance the repair work.

Time.   Fixing up a house can take months of hard, tedious work on your part. Do you have the time? Are you willing to spend it? Remember, with a fixer-upper you could be losing those long weekends to meet with your friends, take trips or simply lounge around watching television. Now, almost every waking moment will be spent fixing up your home.

By the way, it's probably a mistake to think that you'll do the work gradually over many months, or even years. Few people can stand to live in a home that's constantly under construction. The dirt, noise and mess usually force us to get the job done as soon as possible.

This doesn't mean that you can't do it. By making the commitment and setting aside the time, determined people all across the country are successfully saving money by buying and fixing up properties. Yes, it can be done, *if* you're willing to make the sacrifices. The mistake is to believe that no sacrifices are necessary.

Supervision.   Almost no one does all the work fixing up a house single-handedly. You'll be hiring people to work with you. For example, you may want to hire someone to do plastering or electrical work. However, this means that you'll need to make calls to locate the appropriate people. You'll have to be there when they come in to bid the job. You'll have to determine whom to hire. And then, once they begin work, you'll want to supervise to be sure that they do what you want them to do. (On remodeling jobs, watching is critical, because they're not building from scratch. Instead, they're frequently tearing down before they build. You want to be sure they tear down only what you want, not what makes it easier for them to get their part of the job done faster.) Finally, it may mean working with people you don't particularly like.

Supervising actually can be fun. But you need to be able to say yes and no with authority and mean it. You need to be able to make decisions, sometimes quick ones. And you need to be able to live with the mistakes you'll make.

In all honesty, I enjoy this part of fixing up property, having done it many times myself. But I recognize it's not for everyone.

Workmanship.   You would never do a bad job. You know it. I know it. But does the work know it?

What I mean is that a lot of work that you may want to do yourself (either because you like doing it or because you want to save money) requires substantial skill.

Plastering, for example, looks easy to do. You just get a bunch of plaster and slap it on. Except that unless you know trowel techniques, it could end up looking like a mess. Laying tile is similar.

It is possible that only after you do the work will you discover that it didn't turn out quite as planned. What now? Do you rip out and start again? Do you hire a professional to come in and do it right? Do you have the money?

Once again, this problem is not insurmountable. You can buy books that will help you identify those areas where you are most likely to succeed and those where you are most likely to have trouble. (I recommend my own, *The Home Remodeling Organizer*, second edition, Dearborn, 1995.) And you can buy books and take courses to learn how to do skilled work. It's just that you should be aware of this extra and what's involved in getting it done correctly.

A FIXER-UPPER MAY COST AS MUCH AS A FIXED-UP HOUSE

In the final analysis, you have to ask yourself if all of this really pays. When you add in the cost of fixing up and the time and effort spent, do you actually save money over buying a home that's already fixed up and ready to go?

It's probably going to shock many first-time buyers to hear this, but usually you don't save much money. Indeed, unless you buy very carefully, it may cost you more in the long run than it would to buy an already-fixed-up house!

The big reason for this is that property is sold not so much on the basis of the improvement (the house) as on the location (the lot). In really fine neighborhoods, sellers realize that people are willing to do almost anything to get in. So although they may knock the price down a bit if the house is in bad shape, they may not knock it down enough to pay for fixing it up.

In short, in most cases you can't get a fixer-upper cheap enough to warrant doing the work to repair it. On the other hand, having said that, if you're desperate to get into a particular neighborhood, you may be willing to live in a house that's in terrible condition for a long time. If the only way you can get in is a fixer-upper, then the cost comparison really may not matter to you.

HOW DO YOU KNOW IF A FIXER-UPPER MAKES FINANCIAL SENSE?

This is where we get down to the nitty-gritty. It's one thing to think about a fixer-upper in the abstract. It's quite another to actually find a property and then pencil out the figures to see whether it makes financial sense. For the remainder of this chapter, we'll see just how to determine if the fixer-upper you're looking at is a good deal—or a bad one.

Where Is It Located?

For many first-time buyers, the whole idea behind purchasing a fixer-upper is to get into a home in a more desirable neighborhood. Unfortunately, most properties that are suitable for fixing up turn out to be in run-down sections of the city. In fact, if you go to any blighted area of any major city, you will find hundreds, perhaps thousands, of homes that are in really bad shape. The problem, in other words, is that although the fixers are available, they may not be where you want them. In fact, in the more desirable neighborhoods, there may be a scarcity of fixer-uppers. Nevertheless, they do exist in virtually every neighborhood in every city.

Where you need to look is in a prestigious neighborhood in an upscale part of town. What you need to look for is the bad apple in the barrel of good fruit. You want to find a dilapidated, run-down house in a great area.

The problem here is that often savvy sellers of such homes will do the fix-up work themselves, if there isn't too much involved. This means that your chance of finding a house that is just a little run-down but has a significantly reduced price is not very good.

Most sellers realize that the majority of buyers who can afford to purchase a home in a quality neighborhood don't want to buy a house that is going to require a lot of repairs. These buyers want to move into a home that's ready to go. Consequently, if all it takes to get the house into shape is some cosmetic work—painting, recarpeting and a bit of landscaping—the current owner will usually pop for the costs and then sell at full price (the price for which other homes in good condition in the neighborhood are selling).

But don't despair of ever finding a good fixer-upper. Houses that have more than cosmetic problems often don't get fixed up by sellers. If it's going to cost a lot of money to fix up the property—say, more than $10,000 or $15,000—the current owner may not have the funds or may not be willing to commit the time and effort to doing it. He or she may now sell the house "as is." This is your opportunity, if you want a fixer. That's where you come in.

You want to find a house in a good neighborhood that has problems too big for the current owner to remedy easily, but not too big for you. You can then offer a lowball price and have a reasonably good chance of getting it.

Keep in mind that you'll probably be looking for an older home in an older neighborhood. Unless there's some sort of problem with the land itself (such as settling) or poor construction, you probably won't find a newer house as a fixer-upper.

What's the Problem?

Once you accept the fact that to get a fixer-upper at a reasonable price, you're going to have to find a home with more than just cosmetic problems, the next task is to identify the problem and then determine whether you're capable of fixing it. Remember, when a house is priced sufficiently below market to allow you to add in all your costs and still get it for less than a fixed-up property, there is usually something severely wrong with it.

For example, a few years ago a friend was looking for a fixer-upper in a Minneapolis suburb. Most of the houses were in the $200,000 range and were older, some very old. Sharon had determined, however, that this was where she wanted to live and spent several months looking with a number of different real estate agents.

Eventually Sharon found a home with an asking price of $180,000. This was $20,000 below what comparable homes were selling for, but still perhaps $10,000 more than she felt she could afford.

Sharon went back to see the home several times. The walls were full of holes, with bare boards showing through the plaster. The floors were in poor shape, although she recognized them to be hardwood, unusual for the area and probably fixable with just a superficial sanding and finishing. The kitchen and bathrooms were a mess. The real problem, however, was that the beams supporting the roof over the second floor were rotten. The second-floor ceiling bulged downward and looked as if it might soon collapse. It was this problem, in fact, that had thus far scared off all potential buyers. Most figured the house was a total loss.

Sharon, however, called in several contractors to go through the property with her and investigated the possibility of shoring up the roof while replacing the rotten beams. She eventually became convinced that this could be done, figured out how much it would cost and offered the owner $135,000 for the property.

The seller was, of course, outraged, at least on the surface. But he owned the home free and clear, meaning that he didn't have a big loan to worry about when selling. And Sharon was convincing in her arguments that there was a good chance the house would have to be leveled (although she admitted to the seller that she was going to try to fix it). She pointed out that the value of the land alone was only about $100,000, so the seller was getting $35,000 for a potentially worthless home.

Eventually the seller agreed.

Sharon bought the home for $135,000. She had arranged with a bank for a $144,000 mortgage (80 percent of a $180,000 price), with the bank holding back $36,000 in reserve. As Sharon completed her work on the house, the bank would release the money. That was Sharon's fix-up money.

Sharon initially had to borrow on her credit cards to get the repair work started, but as soon as it was complete, the bank would give her her funds and she could pay back her short-term borrowing. At least, that was the plan.

As it turned out, it was easier than Sharon had anticipated. Not all the beams were rotten. Only three were, but they dragged the whole ceiling down. It was a relatively simple matter of replacing them, then replastering and painting. Then she had the floors refinished.

The total cost did not exceed $20,000, so Sharon actually had an extra $16,000 left, which she used to buy a car.

No, of course it isn't going to happen that way every time or even very often. But it can, *if* you use a sharp pencil when figuring your costs, get the property at a low enough price and then get lucky. Which brings us to price.

Pricing a Fixer-Upper

When you check out a fixer-upper, your goal is not to buy for as low as you can get the seller to come down. Rather, your goal is to buy low enough so that you can afford to fix up the property. If the seller won't come down this low, then you're better off looking elsewhere.

Remember, whether a price is too high is a relative thing. Too high for whom? Certainly no price is too high for the seller. The issue becomes whether the price is too high for you, fair though it may seem to the seller.

Here's a formula to help evaluate the fix-up price for any given property:

Purchase price = Resale price - Total costs of fixing - 5 percent

The formula simply says that the price you pay for a fixer-upper plus the total costs of fix-up plus 5 percent for error must equal what you can resell the property for after costs of selling (commission, closing, etc.).

Notice that this formula does not take into account the price the seller is asking for the property. Indeed, the asking price is actually quite irrelevant in a fixer-upper. The only true way to calculate is to determine the price of the property after it is fixed up and work back from there.

Unfortunately, applying the formula is a bit more difficult than simply learning it. To apply the formula, you must determine two difficult-to-determine things in advance:

1. The total costs of fixing up

2. The future resale price

Calculating Your Fix-up Costs

You must take a close look at the project, see what work needs to be done and what can be overlooked. You must also determine what you will do and what you will hire out. And then you must come up with solid figures that have to be pretty close to actual costs.

No, it's not easy to do; but again, it's not impossible, even for a lay person with little to no experience. It just means that you'll need to call in tradespeople to ask their advice and to submit bids.

Locking In the Deal

The problem you'll run into here is that you'll want this information before you lock in the deal (sign a sales agreement). However, the more people in the trades you call, the greater the chances that one or more of them will see the same opportunity and make an offer on the property. At the same time, other people searching for fixers may find this property and be anxious to purchase it before you can finalize your offer.

Therefore, one way to handle this is to use the home-inspection contingency as a tool. Offer what you initially think is the right price, based on whatever information you have. However, insert a contingency clause that says that the deal is contingent on your approving inspections of the property within ten days.

If the seller signs, you now have ten days to check out the property and get estimates on the work to be done. If it turns out that your original offer was in the ballpark, you may simply want to proceed with the purchase. If you were way off, you may now reopen negotiations with the seller. You can point to your estimates from various contractors and indicate that in order to buy, you need a better price. Reopening negotiations after a poor inspection report is done all the time. (Check out my new book, *Tips and Traps When Negotiating Real Estate* [McGraw-Hill, 1995], for more clues on how to handle this.)

The contingency offer is a way to try to get a good deal when you aren't sure of your estimating abilities. It's not the best answer. The best answer is to be a good estimator of costs.

Including a Margin of Error

Note that I included an extra 5 percent so that in case you're a little bit off, you won't get stung. You may want to make it 10 percent, or 3 percent. Just be sure you leave yourself some room for error.

How Much Is Your Time Worth?

This is a hard one to calculate. Most people who look at fixer-uppers simply don't figure in their time. That's a mistake. If you weren't working on the fixer-upper, you could be working at a paying job. Or just relaxing watching television. Instead of doing either of those, you're usually working very hard on the house. Time spent away from another paying job or away from relaxing is important, valuable time. The only question is, how valuable?

There are many ways to calculate this. Perhaps the best I've seen is to apportion a set hourly rate for the time you spend on the fix-up. But do you charge the hourly rate of a professional who could otherwise do the work? Or do you charge a rate for what you yourself could make elsewhere?

My suggestion is to take the higher of the two. You could probably get an extra job and make that money yourself. Or, if something goes wrong, you may need to hire a pro to do the work and pay his or her wage. If you choose the higher, you won't go far wrong.

What About a Profit?

Thus far, we're assuming you just want to recover your costs in a resale. But if you're also interested in investment, as well you should be, your calculation could be far different. On top of your hourly wage, you'll want to add a profit percentage to account for your risk on the deal as well as your return on money actually invested. You may want to add 25 percent. Some investors totally overlook the hourly cost and simply add a percentage, often 10 to 15 percent or more of the purchase price, when calculating what they want to get back on the project.

Determine the Resale Price

Finally, you have to determine how much the property will be worth after you finish fixing it up. This could be the hardest prepurchase task of all. It requires that you make the assumption that the work will be done in good fashion in a reasonable time, and that it will look good to buyers.

The resale price is determined by what comparable homes in good shape are selling for in the neighborhood. For example, let's say similar houses in good shape are selling for $200,000. It's reasonable to expect that the most you're likely to get for your home after fixing it up is $200,000. You may get more because you will have added new features, which buyers like. But not much more. Most people are very concerned about paying extra for overimproved property. (An overimproved home is one into which the owner put too much money, more than is justified by the neighborhood comparables, and now can't get it out.)

This is an important point to understand. For example, let's say that you purchase your home for $170,000 and put in an additional $50,000 to fix it up just right. Is the property worth $220,000? Not if the comparables are going for just $200,000. You can sell your home only for what buyers are willing to pay, and if you overimprove it, you may lose.

But why the emphasis on selling when you're just buying? Because it is the only way you can accurately determine how much to pay. Besides, although you may not intend to sell when you buy, statistics show that people in the United States move around a lot, and you may actually end up selling sooner than you think.

Don't Forget Resale Costs

This next item is controversial. Some experienced fixer-uppers say that you shouldn't worry about the costs of resale, such as agent commission and closing costs. They say that you're going to live in the home for several years, and by the time you get around to reselling, the property should have appreciated enough to cover the costs of the resale.

Maybe. But not all properties have appreciated in recent years. Maybe they will go up—but maybe they won't. I like to figure in the costs of resale as part of my calculations of expenses when I determine the price to pay for a fixer-upper. It may increase my expenses, but at least I know where I stand when I'm finished.

Working Backwards from Resale to Current Purchase.   Let's go over it from the beginning. Remember, to find out how much to pay for a fixer-upper, don't start with the seller's asking price. Start with the resale price, then subtract the costs of fixing up and the costs of sale, plus around 5 percent for error. The result is what you should pay for the fixer-upper.

Calculating Your Purchase Price

Resale price	$_____
Less costs of resale	_____
Less costs of fixing up	_____
Less costs of purchase	_____
Less 5 percent for errors	_____
Purchase Price	$_____

DOES THE BOTTOM LINE MAKE SENSE?

Now step back and take a deep breath. Think for a minute about what we've calculated. We've determined how much to pay for a fixer-upper to be sure it will not cost any more (less costs of resale) than a well-maintained home in the neighborhood—which means you could have bought a fully fixed-up home for about the same price! So why bother?

We've already established the following reasons:

- A fixer-upper can immediately get you into a neighborhood that you might otherwise not be able to afford.

- You will actually be paying yourself, by our method of calculating, because we're tabulating a salary for your time spent.

- You may love it! Many people just love fixing up houses. You may be one of those.

HOW DO YOU FIND A FIXER-UPPER?

Now that you know there are fixer-uppers in almost every neighborhood, as a first-time buyer, how do you go about finding them? Will your broker point them out? Is there a special technique you can use?

Actually, the solution is a little of both. If you tell your agent you're looking for a fixer-upper, chances are he or she will show you anything available in your area and price range. The problem is, however, that many times these properties aren't listed with brokers. Also, many brokers look specifically for homes that are in good condition (to show their prospective buyers). They simply may not have paid attention to the "dogs" in the neighborhood.

As a result, you may have to work with several brokers until you find one who knows fixer-uppers very well. And you may also have to cruise the neighborhood looking for homes being sold by their owner as well as check advertisements in the local paper.

Sometimes owners try to sell the house on their own to avoid paying the sales commission. These houses are called FSBOs (for sale by owners). FSBOs may present a good opportunity, particularly if the house is in terrible shape. A seller may not like the idea of having to sell at a greatly reduced price because of the condition of the property. Rather than list at a lower price *and* pay a commission, the seller may simply be trying save a few bucks by selling on his or her own. Remember, in theory a seller can sell to you for less if there's no agent involved; in practice, however, most sellers plan to save that money for themselves.

Also, conscientiously read the for-sale ads in the paper, both by brokers and by FSBOs. A broker who doesn't want to cooperate with other brokers on the sale of a property may advertise. A FSBO that you have not seen may be listed there. Just get into the habit of reading the classified "real estate for sale" section of your newspaper. If you normally read the front page or the sports or leisure sections, add the real estate classifieds to your reading list. Do it daily. Sometimes you'll go for a month and there'll be nothing. Then an ad may appear, perhaps only for a day or two. If you weren't constantly checking, you'd miss it.

HOW DO YOU GET YOUR PRICE?

Finally, after you've found the house and determined what it's truly worth, how do you get it at a realistic price? Negotiating is almost an art form, but a couple of clues will help.

First, remember that this is not the only home in the world for you. There will be others. If the seller won't consider a realistic price, move on.

Second, offer what you can and make the terms as attractive as possible. The more cash you can put into the deal, the more likely the seller is to believe you are sincere.

Third, never get sentimental when the seller won't budge. Don't say to yourself, "That's the perfect fixer-upper for me. I've got to have it. Let me take out my pencil and paper and see if I can't calculate a little tighter." Don't do that! It's better to lose a house you might have made money on than to buy one on which you will surely lose. If you can't get the right deal, don't monkey with your figures and end up with the wrong deal.

IS A FIXER-UPPER IN YOUR FUTURE?

The problem with searching for a fixer-upper is that it takes a lot of time and patience. It's very easy to give up before you find the right property and a cooperative seller. But just consider that another trade-off. If you want to spend more money, you can buy quickly. But to spend less money, you have to spend more time.

Profiting from Your Home Inspection

CHAPTER 9

Even before the seller accepts your offer on a home, the subject of an inspection is sure to come up. Your agent will want to know if you want to have an inspection clause inserted into the sales agreement/offer. The cost will probably be between $250 and $300, and you'll have to pay for it. Should you have the inspection? Why?

A SAD STORY, BUT TRUE

While home inspections are commonplace today, that was not always the case. Up until ten years ago, very few people had them. In fact, nobody even thought about it. People simply bought homes on the assumption that they were in good shape, or at least that the seller and/or agent would reveal any serious problems.

That was the thinking of a friend of mine, Holli, when she bought her first home, a small, single-family detached house in a semirural community. The house had three bedrooms but only one bath. It was in a quiet, pleasant neighborhood of homes all around 40 years old. It had a lovely front yard and a garden in back. Holli considered it an excellent investment and a place where she and her two children could feel safe and in charge. It was perfect—or so she thought.

The asking price was $115,000. After negotiating, she got it for what she considered a low price of $106,000. She secured an 80 percent loan, and after five weeks the escrow closed and she moved in. That's when her problems began.

The first time she tried to run water in the tub to give her son a bath, it came out orange colored. She turned it off and called a friend, who told her it was probably just rust in the pipes from lack of use. "Let it run for a while and it should clear up." She did, and within a few minutes the water was running clear and warm. Relieved, she continued to fill the tub until she heard a sudden gurgling sound and the tap water slowed to a dribble. Even when she turned the faucets all the way on, no more water would come out. Then she heard her daughter call from the backyard that there was water coming out from the side of the house. She ran out back and sure enough, a puddle was rapidly forming on the side and behind the home, and she could hear the sound of a water spray under the house. She called the water company, and within an hour they had a truck out. By then, her backyard was nearly flooded.

The water company said there was a leak in a pipe under her home. All they could do was turn off the water. She would have to get a plumber to fix it.

Holli and her kids were without water for three days until a plumber could come out and crawl under the house. He said it was flooded underneath and working there would be difficult, but he found the leak and fixed it. He explained that the old galvanized steel pipes under the house were simply rusted away. She could have another leak at any time. He recommended that she replace all the plumbing with copper pipes.

Holding her breath, Holli asked the cost. The plumber said it was only $125 to fix the leak. But it would be about $4,500 to replumb the house, not including patching the holes he would make in the walls. She had to steady herself. She simply didn't have that kind of money.

Holli called the agent, who called the seller. The seller said the house had been a rental, and he hadn't been in it for a year. As far as he knew, there had been no problem with the plumbing before. Besides, the rule was "caveat emptor"—let the buyer beware. Holli should have checked out the plumbing herself. The agent was more sympathetic, but not more helpful. Holli was stuck with the problem.

Three weeks later she had another leak. After that, she took out a second mortgage and had the house replumbed. It was during the replumbing that she discovered the wiring problem.

Forty years earlier when the house had been built, the local building codes had been relatively lax—as, apparently, had building department inspections. The entire house had been wired without a ground wire.

Many people are unaware that all homes today must have three wires coming to each socket. One brings the electricity; the other returns it; and the third is a ground. The ground wire helps to ensure that if there is a short, it will be sent into the ground and not into someone using the socket. It doesn't work all the time, and ground-fault interrupter (GFI) circuits (which break the circuit in the event of a short) are now also required in kitchens and baths as extra protection.

Holli's house was not safe because all of the sockets lacked the ground wire. What's worse, as the plumbers broke into walls to replace plumbing, they saw that the insulation on the wires, an old type of tar mixture no longer used, had broken down and was falling off. They recommended that she have an electrician look at it.

Concerned for her children's safety, Holli called in an electrician who told her that, yes indeed, the house was not up to code. In addition, the wiring had deteriorated and was unsafe. The house should be rewired. The cost would be around $3,500, not including the holes in the walls the electricians made. (Fortunately, all the holes from both the plumbers and electricians could be fixed at once—at a cost of $2,500.)

Holli prepared to get another mortgage. But first she called in a contractor to thoroughly examine the house for any other problems. She found out the roof was old but didn't leak. It would do for now, but would have to be replaced within five years. The water heater didn't leak, but likewise was old and would soon have to be replaced. But there was a leak in the heat exchanger of the furnace, and that would need replacement immediately, at a cost of $1,000. And the yard around the house needed some immediate drainage work for another $600.

Holli arranged for a bigger mortgage and had the problems fixed. Again she called the agent, who talked with the seller. But the seller denied any knowledge of the problems and said, in any event, it wasn't his problem.

Total cost to Holli?

Plumbing	$ 4,625
Electrical	3,500
Plastering	2,500
Furnace	1,000
Drainage	600
Total	$12,225

The house wasn't quite the bargain that Holli had envisioned.

TODAY'S HOME INSPECTIONS

This story occurred about 12 years ago. I doubt it could have occurred today. The difference? Home inspections.

Today every wise buyer will insist on an inspection to check that all of the home's systems are in good shape. If problems are discovered, the buyer can then negotiate with the seller over how to handle them, what should be done and who should pay for it.

To avoid Holli's problem, or anything like it, you should have a home inspection.

GETTING PERMISSION TO INSPECT A SELLER'S HOME

Keep in mind that in today's litigious society, sellers want inspections, too. Sellers don't want buyers to come back after a sale and claim there is a defect in the property that the seller didn't reveal. The buyer could sue for damages, even rescission of the sale. ("Rescission" means the seller would have to take back the property and refund the money.)

I have buyer friends who recently did just that. They bought a single-family detached home in an upscale area. The seller said the house was in perfect condition, nothing but a few minor cracks in the plaster. No damage of any kind. A home inspection likewise revealed nothing adverse.

But when the buyers moved in, they discovered recently patched areas of the foundation that had massive cracking due to earth shifts. Because the sellers had lived in the house for the previous ten years, the presumption was that they concealed the damage and then didn't disclose it. Ultimately, the sellers had to pay more than $15,000 to have the foundation firmed up and for the inconvenience caused to the buyers.

This story has two morals: First, sellers should be forthright; second, inspections aren't perfect. They don't reveal all.

PROBLEMS WITH HOME INSPECTIONS

There are several problems with home inspections. First, the inspection itself is, by its very nature, cursory. You and an inspector (always accompany the inspector; you can learn a great deal by what he or she says as you move through the property) have a couple of hours to look things over. However, during that time there are many areas that you can't really inspect.

For example, if there's wall-to-wall carpeting, it's highly unlikely that you're going to peel it back to look at the floor underneath. If the sellers have patched areas and done a good job with the patches, neither you nor the inspector may catch the fact that they are there (see the story above). In addition, some areas, such as parts of the attic, underneath the house, inside the walls and elsewhere, are simply not accessible.

In short, you can inspect what you can see. That can be a great deal. But it can also leave out a great deal.

Second, the quality of home inspectors, as yet, leaves a great deal to be desired in many parts of the country. Because home inspections are a relatively new development, there has been a rush to cash in on it. An inspector charging $300 apiece can do as many as three inspections a day. If you add it up, that amounts to a very lucrative business. As a result, some people who aren't quite as qualified as they should be have become home inspectors.

Third, the written report, which is the document that says what the inspector has found, too often is simply a printout generated by a home-inspection program on a computer. The inspector simply fills out an entry screen and the computer generates the report. Too often these reports fail to draw any concrete conclusions that the buyer will find useful. (We'll have more to say about this in a moment.)

Finally, our litigious society has come full circle, and today there's a tendency to sue the home inspector for items that weren't revealed (sometimes due to no fault of the inspector). Therefore, inspectors often include many disclaimers and back away from challenging anything that might lead to an angry buyer or seller, sometimes making the report so wishy-washy as to be virtually useless.

A NOT-SO-THOROUGH INSPECTION

An agent I know who was representing buyers asked for an inspection of a home. The inspector came and went. When the inspection report was turned in, it noted several problems, such as leaky faucets, a loose light fixture and some missing shingles. However, it also said that there might be a problem with the foundation, but the inspector could not confirm or deny or this. The same held true for the roof, the walls, the electrical system, the plumbing system, the heating system and the air-conditioning system. In short, anyone—you or I—could have gone through and found leaky faucets and a loose light fixture, and simply looking at the roof would have revealed some missing shingles. But the real nitty-gritty was missing. The inspector simply didn't want to commit to anything more serious for fear of repercussions.

I recently had a similar experience when I bought a home. There was a bulkhead wall in the backyard that was used to keep a hillside from sliding down. I wanted the inspector to tell me the condition of the wall. Was it strong? Would it continue to hold the hillside back for many years? Or was it weak and ready to fall down?

The inspector's report said he could find no damage or problem with the wall, but it could fall down at any time. Now, how useful a statement is that?

All of which means that you may not be getting everything you hope for when you pay for a home inspection.

Many states faced with consumer complaints have begun regulating home inspectors. Today licensing is becoming fairly standard, and soon stiff exams will be in place. Within five years the whole field of home inspection could be as strictly regulated as that for real estate agents. But not yet, in most areas.

How Do You Find a Good Home Inspector?

There is an association called the American Society of Home Inspectors (ASHI). It's a growing organization, and it has some minimum qualifications as well as ethics for its members. I would suggest that anyone you consider as an inspector have membership in ASHI.

In addition, ask for recommendations. The broker with whom you're dealing should be able to recommend a home inspector. But I wouldn't limit myself to one agent's recommendations. Ask another agent or two. The idea is to find an inspector whose name keeps coming up.

Also, call your local building and safety department. Sometimes home inspectors are retired from local building departments. These are the people who regularly go out and inspect property for the city to be sure it meets code. They are well versed in what to look for in a home and have had extensive experience with people who sometimes try to cover things up. Also, these types of inspectors often tend to be more candid than others.

You may also want to consider contractors. People who have retired from the building trades will also sometimes become inspectors. Because of their knowledge of home construction, they can make an excellent choice. However, beware of contractors who wear two hats. If they're both a home inspector and a contractor, they may simply be out scouting for jobs. How will you be able to trust their judgment when they tell you something is wrong, and in the next breath give you an estimate for what it will cost to have them fix it? There's an inherent conflict of interest here.

Structural, electrical and even civil engineers also make good inspectors. I know a home inspector who was formerly a structural engineer. I use him whenever I'm concerned about a foundation or about the structure of a building. He has marvelous insight into how buildings are put together and into diagnosing problems and suggesting cures. On more than one occasion he has told me not to worry about a potential problem I was concerned with, so I went ahead with the deal.

As I said, if after checking the above sources you find the same name popping up over and over again, you may have a winner. Call the inspector up and interview him or her.

YOU DO THE HIRING

You're paying the bill, so you should hire the inspector. Don't delegate this important job to an agent or someone else. Do it yourself. Begin with the interview.

At a minimum, before hiring an inspector I would ask for his credentials. (Did he work in the building department, is he a licensed contractor, in what area, does he have an engineering degree and so on.)

I would also ask for the names of at least three people whose homes he has inspected in the past six months. This should be easy for him to supply, and if he won't, you should ask yourself why. Then I would call each of those people. Find out how the inspection went. Were they satisfied? Did something turn up later that the inspector had overlooked?

BE SURE TO GO ALONG

While the written report is an important part of the home inspection, the verbal discussion as the inspection takes place can be far more important. If you go along, the inspector can point out different things. Along the way you can ask questions about this or that and receive explanations. For example, you might not understand what the inspector means when he says that the vents underneath the home are plugged. If you're with him, however, he'll show you.

But be prepared. Wear old clothing that's warm. Remember, you'll be crawling under the house and in the attic. By the way, don't think that going along is limited to those who are athletic and outdoor types. The softest of women and men these days go along on home inspections. It only takes a couple of hours. But if you're investing $100,000 or more, isn't it worth it?

OBSERVE THE INSPECTOR

One way to judge how good an inspector you have is to observe how he conducts himself. Is he properly dressed for the inspection with coveralls? Does he bring along a flashlight and tools for probing and checking? Is he able to answer your questions logically and clearly? A good inspector should inspire confidence.

ASK FOR A LITERAL REPORT

I don't like those computer-generated reports. It's too easy for the inspector to simply input standard information and, as a result, output a standard report. One report will look much like another. If I'm paying several hundred dollars, I figure the inspector can take the time to write out (or dictate) a literal report. I want it in his or her own words, with specific comments about the house I'm buying.

If the inspector wants to use a computer program, that's okay, but there had better be plenty of sheets at the end with specific comments. Besides, if the inspector has to write everything down, I'm more likely to find out what he or she really thinks.

CAN YOU BLAME THE INSPECTOR?

What if the inspector overlooks something? What if he or she leaves out part of the home? I recently bought a home in earthquake country, and the inspector failed to note that the gas water heater was not tied down. (Water heaters need to be tied down to prevent them from falling over during an earthquake, breaking the gas line and causing a fire.) The inspector came back himself and personally tied down that heater.

Inspectors are liable for their errors, omissions and outright mistakes. The problem is that, to cover themselves, they will often hedge on their answers. As a result, as noted earlier, what you will often get on an inspection report is a lot of banalities and superficial comments about items and conditions that you could have seen for yourself. On the other hand, if there really is a bad condition that's obvious, most inspectors will note it as such. For example, a deck that's about to collapse because the underpinnings have been worn away should be noted and warned against by the inspector.

Also, inspectors will only warrant the home at the time of the inspection. They will stipulate that the report indicates the condition of the house as they found it. Of course, things could be considerably different by tomorrow. And they will include many paragraphs of disclaimers saying that because they didn't see inside the walls or under the carpets, or because the sun was in their eyes, they can't be held responsible for anything they did or didn't find.

In short, even though the inspector is presumably responsible, holding him to an inspection, unless there was some sort of gross problem, is like trying to tie a knot with wet spaghetti. It's pretty darned hard to do.

STEPS TO FOLLOW

Here's what I suggest you do concerning a home inspection:

❏ **Step One:** *Be sure you insist on having a home inspection when you're filling out the sales agreement/offer.* Also, be sure you have a clause making your purchase contingent upon your approval of the inspection. That way you can back out if you need to.

❏ **Step Two:** *Be sure you hire the inspector.* Get recommendations from agents. Check qualifications and interview candidates.

❏ **Step Three:** *Go along with the inspector.* Put on grungy clothes and crawl under that house and into the attic. Ask questions and listen closely to answers. You might even bring along a small tape recorder so you can replay what the inspector said, in case it was confusing at the time.

❏ **Step Four:** *Insist on a literal report with specific comments by the inspector.* Don't settle for a standardized computer printout.

❏ **Step Five:** *Evaluate the report.* If you're not certain about something, ask for an additional inspection. For example, if the roof is noted as having a problem, have a roofer come in and tell you what's wrong and how much it will cost to repair.

Don't be intimidated into approving a bad report. If the inspector finds something wrong, it can be the basis for your backing out of the deal, for getting the seller to pay for repairs or for getting a price reduction.

Your Financing Guide

CHAPTER 10

When you buy a home, whether it be a single-family house, a condo, a townhouse or a co-op, if you're like the rest of us, you're going to need a mortgage. For first-time buyers who usually don't have very much cash to put down and who are stretching to afford the purchase, getting the right mortgage is doubly important. Indeed, it's often the case that the mortgage itself determines what we can purchase.

In Chapter 6, we discussed how big a mortgage you can afford and, as a result, how expensive a home you can manage to buy. In this chapter, we're going to look at the nuts and bolts of actually securing that mortgage. Here you'll find out what every first-time buyer needs to know about real estate financing.

But first, let's get something very basic out of the way. In nearly all cases when you buy a house, you get a *new* mortgage—you don't take over the seller's existing loan. In fact, you can almost always forget about that old loan; there's nothing you can do with it. (As we'll see in the next chapter, in some rare cases it is possible to work with the seller's existing mortgage, but that's not our concern here.)

What we're talking about is going out and getting a brand new loan from a lender so that you can buy your first home (or else you'd have to pay cash!). Let's begin by understanding what a real estate loan really is.

WHAT IS A MORTGAGE?

The term mortgage is both generic and specific. Generically, it is the name for any loan for which the collateral is real estate. Specifically, it is the name for one type of financing instrument (another type being a deed of trust). What's important for borrowers to know about a mortgage generically is their responsibilities and their liabilities under it.

The responsibilities are straightforward: You must make the payments each month and keep the property in reasonably good shape. (Some mortgages call for payments annually or every six months or some other time period, but that is rare.) Also, sometimes the monthly payments do not fully pay off the mortgage. In that case, you are additionally responsible to pay the balance of the mortgage in full when it comes due (called a balloon payment, which we'll also discuss later).

In terms of liabilities, there are penalties if you fail to live up to the mortgage terms. With most mortgages, if you don't make the payment by a certain day, usually two weeks after the payment is due, there is a late penalty, often equal to 5 percent of the monthly payment. (If your monthly payment is $1,000, the late payment penalty is usually $50.) Normally, the lender will not accept a late payment without the penalty. You may make payments late repeatedly, and if you include the penalty, the lender will accept the funds. However, the lender may report you as a habitually late payer to a credit reporting agency.

If you fail to make payments, the lender, at its option, may foreclose. This means that after following legal procedures, the lender can gain title (ownership) to your home and eventually kick you out. Then the lender will usually report that you have lost your property through foreclosure, which may prevent you from getting a new mortgage from any lender in the future.

TYPES OF FINANCING INSTRUMENTS

There are basically three types of financing instruments in common use today, with variations of each. In most cases you will not be given the choice of the type of instrument. Rather, that will be determined by tradition in the state in which you live and by the lender. (It is possible to negotiate one type over another with a lender, but most unusual.) The importance of knowing the differences between mortgage instruments to you as a first-time real estate borrower has to do primarily with how secure your interest is in the home because of the instrument.

The Mortgage

As I noted earlier, in addition to being a generic term, this is also the name of a specific type of financing instrument. A mortgage as a *specific lending instrument* usually gives you the most security you can have while borrowing money on real estate. The reason is that it provides the most difficult path for the lender when it comes to foreclosing on your home.

Before the lender can take your home away through foreclosure, it must go through the judicial system. Called judicial foreclosure, the process requires the lender to present a case to a judge as to why it is entitled to have the property back. The case, of course, is that you didn't make the payments.

You, however, are entitled to appear before the judge and to plead all sorts of extenuating circumstances, from losing your job and, thus, not having the money to pay back the mortgage, to being tricked into signing mortgage documents that you didn't understand and that are unfair.

While in most cases the judge sides with the lender, that doesn't always happen. Sometimes the borrower, through convincing arguments, can delay foreclosure almost indefinitely.

Further, even after foreclosure is granted, you normally have a period of "redemption." During this time, you may redeem the home by paying back all of the money owed on the mortgage along with penalties and lender's actual costs. Depending on the state, this redemption period can extend for several years.

The Deed of Trust

Because of the sometimes lengthy and occasionally uncertain results obtained from judicial foreclosure, lenders over the years developed a different type of mortgage instrument, currently used in most states. The "trust deed" differs from the mortgage primarily in that it need not use judicial foreclosure to take your property back (although that is an option a lender may choose, as we'll see shortly).

Under a trust deed, you actually deed your property over to a third party, a trustee, at the time you secure the loan, along with instructions to the trustee to deed it over to the lender if you fail to live up to the terms (don't make your payments). Don't worry about the trustee; it's usually a title insurance company and is a responsible entity that won't give your property away without good reason.

What this does mean, however, is that when you don't make your payments, instead of going to a judge, the lender simply writes a letter to the trustee saying you're in default. You must be given notice of this default, and unless you can demonstrate that the lender is in error, the trustee will follow a set procedure that ends up with the lender getting a deed to your property and you being ousted.

It's quick and clean, from the lender's perspective—and because of the short time involved and the lack of judicial procedure, not nearly as secure an instrument for you as a mortgage.

However, to avoid misuse, each state has enacted laws that specifically govern how a trust deed may be foreclosed. Most follow the California example. Here, after you have missed loan payments, the lender must give you a notice of default, letting you know that the proceedings have started. You now have 90 days in which to make up all your unpaid loan payments plus penalties and any accrued interest. This is your redemption period. Notice that it comes *before* the foreclosure, rather than after.

If you don't pay up in 90 days, the lender then must advertise the trustee sale of your property for 21 days in a local newspaper. (This is usually a "legal" newspaper read only by those in real estate and law and seldom seen by the average consumer.) During this period you can redeem your property by paying off the loan *in full*. At the lender's discretion, you might also be able to reinstate the loan by paying up back payments.

After 21 days of advertising, the trustee offers your property for sale "on the courthouse steps" to the highest bidder. The lender offers the amount of the loan and is often the only bidder, taking the property back as the trustee issues it a deed. After this you have no redemption opportunities. The property is gone.

Deficiency Judgment.   While there is yet another real estate loan instrument, as we'll see in a moment, both the specific mortgage and the trust deed have two additional aspects in common that need to be commented upon. The first is a deficiency judgment.

If, after foreclosure, the lender is able to sell the property for at least the loan amount plus expenses of foreclosure, meaning the lender can get all of its money back, there is no problem. However, sometimes, particularly in recent years, it's a "short sale." In other words, the lender takes the property back and, when it goes to resell, finds that the property is worth less than the loan—sometimes a lot less.

When this happens, the lender may want to come back to you, the borrower, for the deficiency—the difference between what was still owed on the real estate loan and the amount the home brought on resale.

A deficiency judgment can be issued only by a judge in a judicial foreclosure. Thus, it is a real possibility with a mortgage. It is a slim possibility, however, with a trust deed, *unless* the trust deed lender chooses to foreclose the loan judicially instead of going through the trust deed procedure, which is its option. Sometimes lenders that have a trust deed and believe you personally have a lot of money somewhere will purposely take the longer judicial route to foreclose just for the purpose of later securing a deficiency judgment against you.

The Purchase Money Mortgage.   Nearly all states, however, recognizing that most people who get a mortgage (or trust deed) are simply buying a home and are not sophisticated investors, have instituted purchase money mortgage laws. These simply state that if the mortgage or trust deed was part of the purchase price of the home in which you live, no deficiency judgment is allowed, regardless of whether the lender goes through court. With a purchase money mortgage (any mortgage that was part of the purchase price), you're home free, at least with regard to having a deficiency judgment hanging over your head.

But remember, the loan must be part of the purchase price. If you later refinance, the new loan is no longer part of the purchase price and a deficiency judgment is possible.

Land Contract of Sale

The final financing instrument we'll consider is the land contract of sale, which offers you, the borrower, the least security. Used originally for the purchase of land but now used for any real estate purchase, this is actually not a true loan, but rather a contract to purchase.

The way it works is that you usually give the seller a small down payment (though none is required) and then sign a contract saying that you will pay the seller so much each month, plus interest, either until you've paid off the property or until you've paid enough to equal a full down payment and then refinance.

When you've paid enough to pay off the property or equal the agreed-upon down payment, the seller will give you a deed to the property, providing you come up with conventional financing (a mortgage or trust deed) for the balance. As you can see, the contract of sale is actually an agreement to purchase, but not a purchase in itself.

If you don't make the payments, there is no foreclosure in a contract of sale, because you don't own the property. If you fail to make payments, the seller can have you thrown out.

However, sellers can also change their minds about selling. If that happens, the only way you can force them to actually sell the property to you once the terms of the contract are fulfilled is to go to court—potentially a lengthy and expensive process.

In addition, although many states have added some protections, who's to say that the seller can't give the same contract of sale to more than one person? In other words, a truly dishonest seller could sell the property again and again to different people. (As noted, many states now allow you to record the contract of sale with just your own signature notarized, instead of both, as is normally required. This gives you some protection but not a guarantee.)

Quite frankly, although it can be used successfully by sophisticated investors to achieve certain purchase and tax goals, I would not suggest using a contract of sale for a first-time buyer. Simply stay away if a seller mentions it. Instead, get a mortgage or trust deed, a true sale and a policy of title insurance in your name.

WHERE CAN I GET A MORTGAGE?

As noted in Chapter 6, there are thousands of mortgage lenders spread across the country. They are as close as your nearest bank or savings and loan association. Here is a list of the different sources available to you for a mortgage:

- Banks
- S&Ls
- Credit unions
- Mortgage brokers
- Mortgage bankers

In addition, some insurance companies have occasionally dabbled in direct mortgage lending, and this may be available through a real estate affiliate of the insurance company. Check with your insurance agent to see if that's an option for you.

All of the above lenders offer nearly all of the various types of mortgages that are available and that are discussed in the next chapter. Each, however, usually has its own plans specifically tailored to meet its lending needs.

What this means is that interest rates, points (a fee or prepaid interest equal to 1 percent of the loan per point) and terms will differ from lender to lender. As a first-time borrower seeking to get the best mortgage, you will probably need to check with more than one lender—usually several.

One method of checking is to go to several banks and savings institutions and ask what their mortgage loan programs are. They will be happy to tell you and to give you an application.

While I suggest you inquire of at least one major bank (preferably the one with which you have a checking and savings account, to see if they will give you preferential treatment), investigating numerous lending institutions can be exhausting and may be unnecessary. You can kill several birds with one stone simply by checking with a mortgage broker.

Mortgage Brokers

A mortgage broker is usually a real estate agent specifically licensed by the state to deal in mortgages. He or she is typically a highly sophisticated agent who has long specialized in mortgages and who has contacts with a variety of lending institutions.

Wholesale versus Retail Mortgages. If you think you have a problem as a first-time buyer locating an appropriate lender, think of the problem from the lenders' perspective. They have a variety of mortgage packages that are suitable for different borrowers, some suited exactly to the first-time buyer. Yet how do they find you?

Advertising is expensive and largely impractical. People don't need mortgages on an ongoing basis. They may need one only once every seven to nine years.

Word-of-mouth in the form of recommendations can be effective, but its range is also very limited. What are the chances that one person who gets a mortgage is going to be talking to another who needs one in the near future?

One of the lenders' biggest sources of borrowers actually used to be real estate agents. I can remember some 30 years ago when banks and savings and loans would send representatives around to every real estate office to talk up their programs.

But today there are many more agents, many more offices and many more lenders. And agents are hesitant to recommend a single lender for fear that if the borrower/buyer has a bad experience, it will reflect on the agent.

What was needed was a more efficient system. So lenders began "wholesaling" their mortgages.

To understand the principle behind this, consider buying a pair of shoes in a department store. A department store may carry half a dozen different brands of shoes. When you come in, you have a selection. When you buy, you pay retail.

However, that department store has to make a profit to stay in business. So naturally, it purchases those shoes for less than it sells them to you. It buys them wholesale either directly from the manufacturer or through a wholesaler who sells them in your area.

Mortgages today are handled in a similar fashion. The mortgage brokers are the department stores. They handle mortgages for a variety of lenders—sometimes just four or five, other times as many as 100 or more.

When you walk into the mortgage broker, you pay retail price for your loan. However, to stay in business, the mortgage brokers make a profit on your loan. (Unlike retail stores, however, the mortgage broker doesn't actually buy the loan. He acts as a kind of agent for the lender who provides the funding.) Typically the profit isn't much, often averaging around $1,500. That's the fee a bank pays to a mortgage broker for finding a borrower.

However, in our analogy there were wholesalers that dealt with the department store as well as direct manufacturers. The same holds true with mortgages. Often there are banks in, for example, New England that want to make mortgage loans in California. But they have no way of securing California borrowers. So they will offer their loans through an underwriter that acts as a wholesaler. The underwriter frequently will represent 50 to 100 different lenders. It will secure the commitment to lend money at a certain rate and term and then make it available to mortgage brokers, offering to pay a fee for every borrower found.

An active mortgage broker can offer you mortgages from the bank and the S&L down the street as well as from banks and S&Ls across the country. In addition, insurance companies and other companies that wish to make mortgage loans can likewise form a pool and deal wholesale through the mortgage broker.

Thus, the mortgage broker is your window to the world of real estate finance. He or she can usually offer you the widest possible options when financing.

Can You Buy Wholesale?   Many people, once made aware of how the system works, wonder if they can't save that spread between retail and wholesale. Why can't they go directly to the bank and ask for the $1,500 or so that goes to the mortgage broker?

The answer is that the interest rate, type and terms of a mortgage you can get from bank XYZ directly or from bank XYZ through the mortgage broker are going to be exactly the same for you. The bank will not undercut the mortgage broker by lending wholesale to you.

The reason should be obvious. It's the same reason that a manufacturer won't undercut its retail outlet. If it did, the retail outlet would stop selling its product. If the bank undercut the mortgage broker, the broker would stop finding borrowers for the bank. And, as we saw at the onset, that would return the bank to its original problem of finding good borrowers.

Mortgage Brokers Can Give You Problems

Unfortunately, not all mortgage brokers are created equal. Some work diligently to get the right mortgage for you, the first-time borrower. Others, thankfully in the minority, charge extra fees (on top of what the lender pays them), don't always deliver (the lender refuses to fund at closing) and equivocate on the interest rate and terms. In other words, they cheat.

This is more of a problem during a period when interest rates are low and there are a great many borrowers. This last happened in 1993, when mortgage rates dropped to the high 6 percent level for a short time. Millions of people sought to refinance their homes, in addition to the millions who were buying. There were literally lines of people at mortgage brokers' offices trying to get loans.

This hyper market led to abuses as fly-by-night operators jumped in and even a few established mortgage brokers sought to take advantage of harried borrowers. However, as rates rose to more normal levels, most of the abuses died out, and the worst element left the field.

That doesn't mean, however, that every mortgage broker is going to treat you wonderfully. As a first-time borrower, you have to be on your guard. Try calling on two or three different mortgage brokers. Interview them. See what they have to offer and what they say. Don't sign anything—and in particular, don't give them any money until you're sure which one you want to deal with. (Also ask several real estate agents for recommendations. As noted earlier, they are very concerned that the mortgage broker perform well so that the deal will go through, and may be able to recommend one or two good ones.)

Mortgage Broker versus Mortgage Banker. If you look up mortgage broker in the telephone book, you're going to find the heading is located close to "mortgage banker." What's the difference?

We've already seen what a mortgage broker is. A mortgage banker is a bit different. A mortgage broker lends other people's money to you. A mortgage banker lends its own money. In a sense, it's like a bank.

Yet even that definition is not wholly accurate. A mortgage banker is like a wholesaler acting on the retail level. The mortgage banker usually has several millions of dollars with which to work. And it usually keeps very good track of what's happening in the secondary market.

Remember those pools of out-of-state banks and insurance companies we talked about? They form part of the secondary market. Semiofficial government institutions such as Fannie Mae or Freddie Mac are also part of it, buying mortgage loans from retailers.

Well, the mortgage banker puts together several of what it considers to be highly competitive mortgage plans and then tries to find borrowers like you. When you borrow from a mortgage banker, it will fund the loan with its own money (something a mortgage broker could never do). Then it will take your loan, place it together into a package with a dozen or 100 other loans from other borrowers, and sell that on the secondary market. (Actually, it gets a commitment in advance from a secondary lender, but that's more detail than is necessary for our purposes.) Because it's able to do this, it usually gets a higher return than a mortgage broker.

The benefit to you of dealing with a mortgage banker is that *sometimes*, not always, it can offer you a mortgage with a substantially better interest rate and terms than you can get elsewhere. Calling at least one mortgage banker as you hunt for a real estate loan is a good idea.

A word of caution, however: Some mortgage bankers themselves deal only on the wholesale level; that is, they deal only through mortgage brokers, just like banks. When you call, the first thing you should ask is if they offer direct mortgages to consumers. If not, try elsewhere.

How Should You Speak to a Lender?

Remember, it's business. You're there because you need a mortgage. The lender is there because it needs to loan money. Neither of you is doing the other any favors. It's business. So, even though you're a first-time mortgage borrower, don't go to the lender with your hat in your hand. Walk tall, sit straight and negotiate as equals. It's business.

The person with whom you will deal is often, in reality, a salesperson. He or she may work with you throughout the lending process but may have limited room for maneuverability if you ask for certain fees to be waived, as described later in this chapter. Therefore, it's usually to your advantage to talk directly to the mortgage broker or to a bank/S&L officer. If you ask to do this up-front, there usually isn't a problem, and in the long run you'll get better service.

WHAT SHOULD YOU ASK A LENDER?

Consider your meetings with lenders as an interview. You're interviewing them to see what they have to offer you. Therefore, you naturally want to know what's available that's going to benefit you.

Interest Rate

Of greatest importance is going to be the interest rate. That will determine how high your monthly payments will be. Be careful, however, that you understand the answer the lender gives. The standard for quoting interest rates is for *fixed-rate, 30-year conforming* loans. Be sure that's the quote given to you, so you can use it for comparison with other lenders.

If the lender begins quoting you its rates on adjustable mortgages, you'll have a much more difficult time comparison shopping. Each lender's adjustables are going to be slightly different; the rates quoted, therefore, will be like comparing apples with oranges.

To get a good idea of what interest rates really are at the time you're looking for a mortgage, you can check at least two independent sources: your local paper and real estate agents.

Many large city newspapers list the current interest rate for mortgages charged by the largest lenders in the area. Typically, this will appear in the real estate section of the Sunday paper.

Often, large real estate offices will print up a list of interest rates charged by various lenders and make it available to clients. Sometimes this list is published by local escrow or title insurance companies. Find out who has the list and get a current copy.

132 Buy Your First Home!

Annual Percentage Rate

You should be aware that the APR (annual percentage rate) is going to be different from the rate quoted by the lender. The APR required by truth-in-lending laws demands that the lender include all costs. That means that the points and other costs are added in when determining the rate. The interest rate usually quoted on mortgages, however, is just the rate on the interest, not the additional costs.

Both figures are useful. The quoted rate usually tells you the interest rate that will be used to determine your monthly payments. The APR tells you the true rate you will pay, based on all costs. Use the APR when comparing different types of mortgages. Use the quoted rate when you want to know what your monthly payments will be.

Points. You'll also want to ask how many points the lender charges for the mortgage. Remember, a point is equal to 1 percent of a loan. One point for a $110,000 mortgage is equal to $1,100.

Often the points will be on a sliding scale, depending on the interest rate. If you are willing to accept a slightly higher interest rate, your points should be lower. On the other hand, if you pay more points, you should get a lower interest rate. For example, if you're quoted 8.5 percent at two and a half points, you might also be able to get 8.25 percent at four and a half points, or 8.7 percent at half a point. (The relationship of points to interest rate varies between $1/8$ and $1/4$ percent in interest for each point.)

Terms. You will also want to know what the terms of the mortgage are. Are there any balloon payments (where it all becomes due and payable on a certain date)? If it's an adjustable-rate mortgage, what are the steps, the margin, the index and other features? (These are explained in detail in the next chapter.) In short, you want all the other data about the mortgage so that you can determine if it's good for you.

Fees. There are always fees that lenders charge. You will be presented with a list of these as soon as you formally apply for a mortgage, but it's a good idea to ask about them up-front. That way, if they seem unwarranted, you won't waste a lot of time and can quickly go elsewhere.

Here are the normal fees you can expect to be quoted:

- *Credit Report Fee* — Usually under $50.

- *Property Appraisal Fee* — Usually $250 to $400.

- *Loan Application Fee* — For processing your application— $250 to $400; may be waived by direct lenders, such as banks or S&Ls.

- *Points* (explained above)

- *Tax and Insurance Escrow Fee* — Used to set up an impound account that allows the lender to pay your semiannual taxes and your annual fire (or homeowner's) insurance on a monthly basis. It significantly increases your monthly payment, but it's a good idea to have this for first-time buyers, as it means you won't have to worry about coming up with big tax and insurance bills. It is required on all mortgages with a down payment of less than 20 percent. It is not usually required on mortgages with a down payment of 20 percent or more. (The set-up fee is usually under $100.)

- *Lender's Title Insurance Policy* — An extra policy that protects the lender. (Cost depends on the value of the property.)

- *Interest Proration* — The interest accrued between the time the mortgage is funded and the time the first month's interest begins. (Interest on mortgages is paid at the end of the month, unlike rent, which is paid in advance.)

Sometimes borrowers are charged additional fees that have become known in the trade as "garbage" fees. These are extras thrown in to pad the lenders' profits on a loan. They are found most often when dealing with mortgage brokers, less often with direct lenders, such as banks. They may include the following:

- *Document Fees* — Anywhere from $50 to $300. It takes virtually no time or effort for a computer to spit out documents these days; therefore, these fees are often unwarranted.

- *Underwriter's Fee* — Usually around $300. This is to cover the lender's cost for selling your mortgage on the secondary market. However, that is a normal part of doing business, and you shouldn't be charged for it.

- *Loan Origination Fee* — Up to one point or more. Some loans (FHA, for example) do have a legitimate origination fee. Conventional loans, however, do not. It is just an additional way of garnering money. The lender should ask either for points or for an origination fee (they amount to the same thing). If the lender asks for both, it's probably unwarranted.

- *Loan Processing Fee* — Anywhere from $75 to $350. Again, this is asking you to pay for the lender's normal costs of doing business. It is usually unwarranted.

- *Commitment Fee, Lock-in Fee, Loan Evaluation Fee,* etc. — These go by a variety of names. Most are garbage fees, just thrown in to increase the cost of the mortgage to you.

SHOULD YOU NEGOTIATE FEES?

Absolutely! Challenge any fees you're not sure of. Ask the lender if they're normal and standard. Then ask another lender in the area the same question. By interviewing three lenders, you can quickly determine which fees are unwarranted.

Then go back to or call the first lender and ask if it is willing to drop these fees if you take the mortgage. Explain that other lenders aren't charging them. You may be surprised at how far lenders will bend to get your business, especially in a tight market.

Lock-ins. These are used to hold a quoted interest rate for a set period of time to allow you to obtain a mortgage. Lock-ins are common in markets where interest rates are rising. You may be quoted 9 percent, for example, but are worried that during the month or so it takes to close the deal, the rates may rise to 9.5 percent or higher.

In this situation, you can ask the lender to lock in your rate. This supposedly guarantees that within the lock-in time frame, you'll get the rate you were originally quoted. However, if rates jump, some lenders won't honor their own lock-in. For example, suppose you're quoted 8 percent and the mortgage market rates jump to 9 percent. To fund you at 8 percent means the lender will have to make up the 1 percent difference. Faced with this, some lenders will conveniently forget about your lock-in.

Therefore, it is a good idea to get the lock-in in writing. However, even this is no guarantee with an unscrupulous lender. For example, a written lock-in may only be for 40 days. You get everything ready so you're able to fund within 39 days. But the lender happens to lose a document "in the mail" until day 41—and suddenly your lock-in doesn't count anymore.

Some lenders charge a fee for a lock-in. I believe this is usually a waste of your money. If rates don't change, you get your mortgage at the quoted interest rate and the lender pockets the lock-in fee. If rates do change, an unscrupulous lender may not go forward with funding the loan, claiming delays, as noted above, and perhaps re-funding your lock-in fee. The only person who loses here is you.

WHAT HAPPENS NEXT?

Once you've found a lender with which you feel comfortable, you are ready to proceed with the mortgage. The lender will give you a lengthy mortgage application to fill out and ask that you bring it back with a check for a credit report and an appraisal. You'll also be asked to bring in certain documentation proving your income, employment and cash holdings.

When you complete the application, but before returning to the lender, *make several copies.* The reason is that most lenders use a standard form accepted by the major underwriters, such as Fannie Mae or Freddie Mac. If it later turns out that you don't want to go with this particular lender, you may not have to fill out another form for a second lender—it will already be done! (Once you see how long and complicated the form is, you'll understand why this is a good idea.)

The documentation you'll be asked to bring in can include any or all of the following:

❏ Paycheck stubs

❏ Two years of federal income tax returns

❏ W-2 tax forms

❏ Copies of statements from your bank (You'll need these for each bank listed in your application and specifically for the bank from which you'll withdraw the money for the down payment. If you have several banks, you may want to list only the ones in which you keep most of your money.)

❏ A list of any other names you've used, as well as a list of all your previous addresses going back at least seven years

❏ A copy of the sales agreement and any signed counteroffers or addenda

❏ A copy of divorce papers

❏ Your actual Social Security card and your driver's license or other photo ID

❏ A copy of a recorded "satisfaction of judgment," if any

❏ A copy of the sales agreement if you are selling a residence at the same time you're buying a new one

❏ Proof that any previously owned real estate was sold and your old mortgage paid off

❏ Any other documents the lender or insurer may request

Lenders frequently say they have everything they need, only to call back a week later and demand some other document. What has happened is that they prepared a complete package and sent it on to the underwriter, who found something wanting. Now they're coming back to clear up that problem. Act quickly to get them the additional documents, if you want the mortgage.

GET A "GOOD FAITH ESTIMATE"

Under RESPA (Real Estate Settlement Procedures Act), the lender is required to give you an estimate of your costs within three days of the time you make a loan application. (You'll probably be given the form at the time you bring in your completed application.)

Usually, all the items you've previously discussed with the lender will be on this form, along with an estimate of their costs. If the lender agreed to waive a particular charge and it appears here, challenge it. Also keep in mind that the costs listed are *estimates*. They may go up (but rarely down) by the time the loan funds and the deal closes.

WHAT IF YOU HAVE A CREDIT PROBLEM?

The truth of the matter (regardless of what fly-by-night credit "fixers" say) is that you need lots of good credit to obtain a mortgage. That means you need to have borrowed and promptly repaid many loans, such as personal, auto and credit card loans, in the past. You also need to have an excellent history of prompt payment of all your bills (utility, gasoline, rent, etc.).

Even just a couple of late payments can mean you won't get a mortgage, or at least a good "conforming" loan. A default on payments, bankruptcy or foreclosure can preclude you getting almost any financing. (But you may still be able to get seller financing or an assumption—see the next chapter.)

You can't fix bad credit, if you have it. Before a mortgage is funded, the lender checks with all three of the national credit bureaus (TransUnion, Equifax and TRW). If there's a problem, it will show up.

You can, however, sometimes explain problems away. If there's a mistake, and you have written documentation to prove it, that will remove the blemish. Or, you may be able to point to extenuating circumstances, such as that you were ill or laid off at the time. This won't necessarily get you the new mortgage, but it can help.

On the other hand, if you're a first-time buyer who really has made late payments, defaulted on loans or had your auto repossessed, you're simply not going to be able to get a new real estate mortgage. (Again, check on seller financing and assumptions in the next chapter.)

Maintaining good credit is vital in our economy, where what you can buy often depends more on your credit rating than on the amount of cash in your pocket.

Selecting the Right Mortgage

CHAPTER

There is an alphabet soup of mortgages out there. According to one estimate from a large mortgage banker, at one time in the late 1980s there were close to 700 different mortgage variations available nationwide!

Granted, most of these fall within a few broad categories. Nevertheless, as a first-time buyer, you're up against a daunting task in learning which mortgage is the best for you. Indeed, with so many different mortgage opportunities, you might let the best slip by because you were simply unaware that it existed.

In this chapter we're going to try to remedy that. We'll cover more than a dozen of the most frequently used mortgages along with their major variations. However, rather than simply list them randomly, we're going examine these mortgages in terms of their benefits to you. There are five major headings in this chapter:

1. Low Down Payment Mortgages

2. Low Monthly Payment Mortgages

3. Easy Qualifying Mortgages

4. Jumbo Mortgages

5. Special Situation Mortgages

Naturally, there will be some overlap. However, if you're a first-time borrower, this organization should help you to quickly select the mortgage category that will benefit you the most.

LOW DOWN PAYMENT MORTGAGES

Because coming up with cash is usually the hardest part of most real estate purchases, let's consider those mortgages that allow you to put up the minimum down payment. All of these mortgages (with one exception, as we'll see) involve having some sort of insurance or guarantee of your performance. In other words, you get away with less down, because a portion of the mortgage is guaranteed.

FHA Mortgages

These are mortgages that are insured by the Federal Housing Administration (FHA). From the first-time buyer's perspective, they are desirable because the standard down payment is only 5 percent. (In some rural areas and under special programs, that can go as low as 3 percent.) This means that if the house you're purchasing costs $100,000, you only have to come up with $5,000 as a down payment. I'm sure that warms the heart of many readers. However, read on. There are restrictions and negatives about this mortgage.

Maximum mortgage amounts differ from community to community based on the median prices of homes in the area. (The maximum loan amounts change frequently but are rarely very high, meaning these loans would not be very useful in high-priced areas like California or New York.) If your house is much above the medium price or you're in a high-priced area, an FHA loan may not be of much use to you.

In addition, the loan itself is expensive. There is a loan origination fee and usually additional points to pay plus a hefty mortgage insurance premium. In the past, this could be paid monthly as a nominal amount with your regular mortgage payment. However, because so many FHA mortgages went into foreclosure in the 1980s, the government changed its policy and insists that the mortgage premium be paid up-front in a lump sum. (The mortgage can be increased by this amount, however, so you don't have to come up with it in cash.) Also, the government requires strict credit and income qualifications from applicants. And not only the borrower but the house as well must pass a special FHA inspection.

One of the additional benefits of an FHA mortgage is that it is partially assumable. I say partially because the new buyer must qualify for the mortgage in order to assume it. (In the old days, anyone could simply take over an FHA loan without any qualifications.)

FHA loans are available from banks, S&Ls and mortgage brokers. Just ask about them and almost anyone in the lending field can explain how they operate and if they are a viable option in your area.

VA (Veteran's Administration) Mortgages

This is a mortgage that is guaranteed (as opposed to being insured like the FHA loan noted above) by the Department of Veterans Affairs in Washington, D.C. It is available only to veterans of the U.S. Armed Forces who were on duty for a set number of days during specific periods of time. You must check with the VA to see what those dates are, as they are occasionally changed, and obtain a certificate of eligibility.

If you are a qualified veteran, this can be an excellent loan for you, because no down payment is required (although you may pay something down if the house costs more than the maximum mortgage amount). In other words, if the home costs $90,000, your down payment is zero!

Additionally, the buyer cannot pay any points for the mortgage, meaning the seller has to pay them. This is another boon for you; however, it's often difficult to find sellers who are willing to pay your costs. All that's necessary for the buyer to pay are some nominal closing costs.

There are, however, a couple of drawbacks. First, the VA guarantees only a small percentage of the mortgage (the first monies the lender is likely to lose) and up to maximum amounts. (These maximums changes frequently—check with the VA for current amounts.) This means that, as with an FHA loan, you will probably find a VA loan helpful only in less expensive areas of the country.

Second, you are personally held responsible for the payment of the mortgage. If you default and lose the house to foreclosure, you are still responsible to the VA for all the money it pays out as part of its guarantee to lenders.

Third, although these loans are fully assumable to anyone, you are not always relieved of your liability to the VA when you sell on an assumption! If the subsequent buyer defaults, you are still liable for any losses the VA suffers. To avoid this future liability, you must either pay off the mortgage when you sell or get a "release of liability" from the VA. The VA, however, normally won't give this unless the next buyer is also a veteran and assumes liability for the mortgage.

VA loans are available from most lenders, such as banks and S&Ls. However, there is a fair amount of paperwork involved, and some lenders prefer not to issue them. Also, the fact that the buyer can't pay any points, down payment or many fees also makes them a less desired loan for many lenders.

Insured Conventional Mortgages (PMI)

As we noted in Chapter 6, the standard conventional loan is 80 percent of either the appraised value or the selling price, whichever is lower. However, lenders can increase the amount borrowed to 90 percent or even 95 percent in some cases, provided you are an excellent credit risk *and* there is private mortgage insurance (PMI) on the loan.

PMI came into existence about 20 years ago as a way for conventional (non-government-insured or -guaranteed) lenders to offer low down payment loans—as low as 5 percent, as noted above. The insurance comes from private companies and covers the first 20 percent of the mortgage. In other words, if you default and the lender takes back the property and then is unable to sell it for the mortgage amount, PMI will cover up to the first 20 percent of the lender's loss. In most cases, this is the entire loss by the lender.

Again, for you, the borrower, this is an opportunity to come up with a low down payment mortgage. However, there are some off-setting features. First, there is a PMI premium that must be paid each month. This is usually between one-fourth and three-eighths of 1 percent and is added to the regular interest rate, thus increasing the monthly payment. In other words, if your interest rate is 8 percent, with PMI it may now become 8.25 percent.

On the good side, however, if you stay in your home long enough to make monthly payments to equal 20 percent *of the original purchase price (or to have your house appreciate that much in value)*, you can have the PMI insurance cancelled and save that extra quarter percent or so.

Unfortunately, some unscrupulous lenders have been cancelling PMI on properties that either have obviously appreciated in value or have had mortgages on them long enough to equal the 20 percent down, and then kept the premium the borrower was paying each month for themselves! This has reached the level of a national scandal, and there are efforts afoot to require lenders to refund that portion of the monthly payment that goes to PMI when the insurance is cancelled.

To get the lender to cancel insurance on your property if you have PMI, you must pay for a new appraisal and an evaluation of your payment history. Even then, this is such a lucrative source of income that many lenders still refuse to cancel the PMI.

Any private lender will usually offer some PMI mortgages. But you will have to have sterling credit and a strong income to qualify. Plus, the property must be in a choice area with strong resale potential.

In short, PMI is not a panacea. But for some first-time buyers, it can be a wonderful way to get in with little down.

Seller Financing

This is the oldest method of getting a small down payment on the books. Here, in addition to a new mortgage that you get from an institutional lender, you get a second mortgage from the seller. For example, you get an 80 percent loan from the bank and the seller lends you an additional 15 percent. You now can get the property with as little as 5 percent down, plus closing costs. And there is no qualifying for the second mortgage, because it's coming from the seller! (We'll have more to say about that feature shortly.)

The problem here is that very often sellers do not want to give mortgages because of the risk involved (you might not repay) and because they need the cash to buy another property. Thus, while you can sometimes find a seller who will "carry back" some "paper" (as these loans are called in the trade), it is not that often.

The amount of the second mortgage is between you and the seller. However, today many sellers are wary of anyone who wants to put less than 10 percent cash down. The reason is that a few years ago, some real estate gurus were advocating that buyers purchase homes with nothing down by getting the seller to finance the entire down payment. In return, the seller usually received a higher price.

However, in the long run, many of these investment buyers defaulted, and the sellers were forced to go through the time, expense and anguish of taking back their properties and trying to resell. Often they lost everything. Today, therefore, sellers are wary of this "creative financing."

Additionally, today many institutional lenders will set not only a maximum loan amount, but also a maximum *combined* loan amount. That means that while you may get 80 percent of the price from the lender, that same lender will allow you to borrow only 10 percent from the seller for a combined total of 90 percent.

There are additional methods of creative financing that do work; however, they are beyond the scope of this book.

LOW MONTHLY PAYMENT MORTGAGES

Thus far we have examined mortgage types that help the first-time buyer get into a home with a lower down payment. Now let's consider some different types of mortgages, specifically designed for lower monthly payments. (Note that some of the following can be combined with low down payment mortgages. For example, you can combine an ARM with a PMI mortgage.)

ARM (Adjustable-Rate Mortgage)

An ARM can cut your mortgage payment by a third or more, at least in the early days of the mortgage. For example, if your payment were $900 a month with a fixed-rate mortgage, an adjustable-rate mortgage could initially cut that down to $600 a month or even less.

This has two important ramifications, especially for first-time buyers. First, with a lower monthly payment, you may be able to get into a house and a neighborhood that you would not otherwise qualify for. Second, because you're making a lower monthly payment, it will be easier for you to maintain a higher-quality lifestyle.

On the other hand, ARMs have some very significant drawbacks. The most important of these is that the low monthly payment lasts only a relatively short time—months or, at the outside, a few years. After that, the monthly payment usually rises very quickly to a point where it's actually higher than if you had opted for a fixed-rate mortgage!

Good for the Short Term. Therefore, the ARM is particularly useful if you're planning on living in the home for only a short period of time—say, three years or less. During that time you should save a considerable amount on monthly payments compared to a fixed-rate mortgage.

And the ARM is also useful during periods of temporarily high interest rates. The ARM allows you to get into a property at a lower rate when market rates are high. Then, after several years when, presumably, rates have fallen, you can refinance to a lower-rate mortgage.

Those are the benefits and the reasons for getting an ARM. If it's appealing to you, let's consider how it works.

The reason an ARM can offer lower-than-market interest rates is that, unlike with a fixed-rate mortgage, the interest rate fluctuates. Actually, it's tied to a financial index (that the lender can't control) and moves up and down as that index moves up and down.

Teasers.   However, the key part of this arrangement is that when you first get the mortgage, there is a very low "teaser" rate. This rate, which is designed to get you interested and hooked on the mortgage, may be less than half of the market rate! For example, the going rate for mortgages could be 9 percent, yet a lender's teaser rate may only be 4 percent. That means that the payments for the ARM, at least initially, are going to be less than half the payments on a fixed-rate mortgage. That's a lot of incentive.

The problem is that the teaser rate doesn't usually last very long—typically never longer than six months, and sometimes as short a period as one month. After that, the interest rate begins to "adjust" to market conditions: It rises. And it continues to rise at set adjustment periods until it's at (or usually slightly above) market rate.

For example, let's say the adjustment periods are every three months and the steps are 1 percent. (A "step" means the maximum adjustment that can be made during the period.) The progression would look like this:

Teaser Rate	3 months	6 months	9 months	1 year
4%	5%	6%	7%	8%

The mortgage that starts out at 4 percent can very quickly double in interest until, at the end of the year, you may be paying twice as much!

Indexes and Margins.   How high the interest rate can go is determined by the index used and the margin. Common indexes include T-Bill rates, federal funds rates and even LIBOR (London Interbranch Bank Borrowing) rates. For example, let's say the index is at six. The lender now arbitrarily tacks on a margin—say, three; that gives you your adjusted interest rate, as follows:

Calculating an ARM Interest Rate

Index + Margin	=	Your interest rate
6 + 3	=	9

Obviously, if the index goes down, so too will your interest rate. But if the index goes up, your interest rate also will increase.

Further, at the beginning of your mortgage, when you have your teaser rate, your true interest rate will be much higher. For example, your teaser may be at 4 percent, but your true interest rate may be at 9 percent. That means that each adjustment period, your rate will rise the maximum step until it reaches 9 percent.

However, it will continue on up for a period (under some ARMs) until you make up the interest lost by the lender when your rate was below market! In short, you don't gain anything in the long run and may indeed lose. But if you sell quickly before the rate rises, you could save a great deal.

Caps. In addition, many ARMS offer caps on the interest rate. This means that the interest rate may not rise beyond a certain maximum. The cap is typically 4 percent to 6 percent above the current market interest rate, so there's relatively little chance the mortgage will get that high (unless there's suddenly runaway inflation in the country). The cap is a "feelgood" sort of thing, but it's rarely going to be helpful.

Other mortgages offer caps on the monthly payment. They guarantee that the monthly payment will not rise beyond a certain point. Again, this is designed to make you "feel good" about taking the mortgage. The problem is that if the interest rate rises to the point where the monthly payment should be higher than the cap, the difference that you're not paying is usually added onto the loan amount. Further, because it's added to the mortgage amount, you pay interest (on that interest) in the future! This is called negative amortization and should be avoided by first-time buyers. It is a perfect definition of an "ugly mortgage."

ARMs are complex mortgages, and of necessity the description here is brief. They are a real boon to first-time buyers, and you should seriously consider them. But you should also take into account their drawbacks. For more information on ARMs, read my book *Tips and Traps When Mortgage Hunting* (McGraw-Hill, 1992).

GPM (Graduated Payment Mortgage)

This type of mortgage was designed specifically for the first-time homebuyer. It has a low initial interest rate with steps at designated periods of time (usually every year or so) that raise the interest rate and monthly payments at predetermined amounts. Eventually, perhaps seven years down the road, the interest rate ends up higher than the market rate when you made your purchase.

The idea here is that as you get older and, presumably, your income grows, so too will the mortgage payment. You will have low payments when you first start out, and then, as you're (one hopes) more able to pay, you'll pay more.

Unlike with an ARM, where the mortgage adjusts according to an index and it is impossible to know what the future payments will be, this is a fixed interest rate mortgage, only the rate changes at predetermined times and for a predetermined amount.

If you see yourself on a career course that will provide you with increasing income, this could be a good mortgage for you. The problem, of course, is that the payment schedule is inflexible, and if your career nosedives, you might not be able to make that ever-higher monthly payment, and you could lose your house.

On the good side, however, you never have to worry about negative amortization with a GPM. And you won't get any shocks. You'll know well in advance what every monthly payment will be.

GPMs are often combined with FHA mortgages. Ask your lender for more information about them in your area.

Convertible Mortgages

This is my favorite type of mortgage and the one I most often recommend to first-time buyers. It combines the best of the adjustable-rate with the best of the fixed-rate mortgage. Here's how it works.

The mortgage has two different time periods: an initial loan period and then a secondary loan period. Although the terms can vary greatly, generally during the initial time period you have a lower-than-market fixed-rate mortgage. During the secondary time period, you have a rather ugly adjustable-rate mortgage.

For example, the current market rate may be 8 percent. You get a three-year convertible mortgage. That means that during the first three years of your mortgage, your payments may be based on a 7 percent interest rate amortized (paid in equal payments) over 30 years, just as if you had a true 30-year, fixed-rate mortgage. You save 1 percent for the three years.

At the end of year three, however, the mortgage usually converts to an adjustable-rate mortgage with a high margin and a volatile index, and you usually end up paying more than market interest rate.

Convertibles as described above are available in a variety of terms, the most common being three, five, seven and ten years, all amortized over a 30-year period. They are sometimes called by their term— 3/30, 5/30, 7/30 and so on. The shorter the initial fixed interest rate period, the more you save on your mortgage.

The advantage here is that you know in advance what your monthly payment will be for a fixed period of time. If you're like most people, you'll probably plan to sell before that time period ends, and hence you get the benefits without incurring the drawbacks (the high interest rate adjustable).

There are a number of variations on the convertible, the most common being a mortgage that starts out as a rather pleasant adjustable with a good index, reasonable margins and fair steps. However, at a certain point, usually between years three and five, you have the one-time option of converting it to a fixed-rate mortgage at the then-current interest rates.

Interest Only

One of the more recent entries into the home mortgage field and a possibility for a first-time homebuyer is the interest-only loan. This is a fixed-rate mortgage. As its name implies, instead of paying back interest plus principal each month, you pay back only interest.

However, because of the mathematics of amortization (payback) of loans, this is only a small savings, perhaps in the neighborhood of less than 5 percent of the monthly payment. (Most of the interest is paid at the beginning of the mortgage, most of the principal repaid at the end.)

If you're not planning to keep the property long and want a slightly lower fixed interest rate mortgage, this is another option.

Balloon Payment Mortgage

This type of mortgage will sometimes earn a first-time buyer a lower interest rate and, therefore, a lower payment. But beware: You could end up losing your house if you don't take timely action.

A balloon mortgage is any type of mortgage that is not fully amortized, which means it does not pay itself off in equal payments. Typically such a loan will be for a fairly short number of years—say, five—during which you make interest-only payments. At the end of that time, the mortgage is all due in one huge (balloon) payment.

EASY QUALIFYING MORTGAGES

Thus far we've been discussing mortgages that allow you to buy with less money down and those with a lower monthly payment. Sometimes the issue is not payments or cash, however, but credit. Sometimes because of a bad credit history, or because you don't have a strong income, you cannot qualify for the types of mortgages we've been describing. Again, this is frequently the case with first-time borrowers who are often in the process of establishing their credit and growing their careers. There are several specific options available to you.

Seller Financing

We already touched on this earlier. However, it bears some extra consideration for first-time buyers who have trouble qualifying.

When a seller gives you part of a home's (it can be a house, condo, townhouse or co-op) purchase price in the form of a mortgage, there's usually little to no qualifying. Oh, you may have to submit a credit report to the seller, but usually that's it. Compare that to the extensive documentation, minimum income and good credit required by an institutional lender. You'll quickly see that this is a great way to get easy financing.

The trick is to find a seller who's willing and able to do it. A fair number of sellers will help out by taking back a second mortgage, but usually not for more than 10 percent of the sales price. Remember, they usually need the cash to buy another house themselves, and often they owe a lot on their own mortgage.

So, if you're a first-time buyer with a problem qualifying for a new mortgage, it would behoove you to spend some time going through a broker's listings looking for sellers who either have their property paid off or have a small mortgage on it. If their property is paid off, they might give you a mortgage for 80 percent or more of the price; or maybe they could give you a 20 or 30 percent mortgage, and you could get an institutional first mortgage for 50 or 60 percent (far easier to qualify for).

Why would a seller do this? Sometimes sellers don't want cash—they want income. And mortgage interest is usually among the highest long-term interest paid. A retired seller might see you as the perfect solution to his problem!

Remember, this is a long shot. You won't find many sellers both with a lot of cash in their property and who are willing to help finance. But they do exist. Just remember, however, that you won't be able to be as picky in terms of the neighborhood or the house.

Assumable Mortgages

Another way to avoid qualifying difficulties is to find a house that already has a big assumable mortgage on it. "Assumable" means that you can take it over.

Most modern mortgages are not assumable. That means that when the current borrower sells the home, he or she must pay off the mortgage; the new buyer can't assume it.

But a few mortgages are still assumable. Many of these are ARMs, older FHA mortgages (over ten years old) and VA loans. The newer FHAs and most of the ARMs still require some qualifying, but usually it's not as strict as when you go for a brand new loan. And there's still an occasional old-fashioned, fully assumable loan to be found here and there.

Buying "Subject To"

When you tell an agent about your problem qualifying, the topic of buying "subject to" is sure to come up as a possible solution. What this means is that you buy a property without either assuming the existing mortgage or paying it off. You treat it, in fact, as if it isn't there, sort of.

What happens is that the seller "forgets" to tell the lender that the property was sold and you continue to make payments on the seller's mortgage. You record the deed in your name after making the down payment and take possession. It's a legitimate sale—but it's not legitimate financing.

If the lender ever finds out (which in reality happens only about 50 percent of the time, when notice of the deed being recorded to someone else is forwarded to the lender), it may immediately begin foreclosure to take back the property ... or not. As long as the payments keep rolling in, particularly when there's a depressed housing market, the lender may simply choose to look the other way. (One form of this is called a "wrap," or wraparound, in which several mortgages may be included.)

Obviously, this is not a course recommended for the faint of heart. You could quickly lose your home and your down payment.

JUMBO MORTGAGES

These are very big mortgages that are frequently found in high-cost areas.

Conforming Loans

Even though I haven't emphasized it, what we've mostly been talking about thus far are conforming mortgages—those that are below the underwriter's limits for sale in the secondary market, currently set at $203,400. (The maximum amount changes frequently, so check with a lender.) Whether the lender actually disposes of this mortgage in the secondary market is not really relevant. It's that the mortgage qualifies to be sold to the secondary market.

However, perhaps you're living in an area where housing prices are considerably higher than the conforming maximum. In some cities in California, for example, you can't buy the cheapest house with a $203,400 mortgage. What do you do when you need a jumbo loan?

I suspect that those who are looking for jumbos are going to be in the minority of first-time buyers. Nevertheless, they are worth mentioning if for no other reason than so you'll know what the lenders are jabbering about when they mention them.

Any mortgage above the secondary market limit is considered a jumbo. It's made by an individual lender (usually a bank or S&L), not sold on the secondary market, and can be for any amount up to and over $1 million. (It is also sometimes called a portfolio mortgage, meaning the lender keeps it in its own portfolio of loans.) These mortgages carry slightly higher interest rates (depending on the qualifications of the buyer), and for that reason, lenders love them. Money is money, and this way they get more interest on it.

If you need a jumbo, check with a bank or S&L in your area, although some mortgage brokers do handle them, too. Loan programs vary enormously and sometimes can be set up specifically to meet your needs. These are really custom loans tailored for specific needs and properties.

SPECIAL SITUATION MORTGAGES

There are a number of other mortgage types that are used for special situations. I don't recommend any of them for a first-time buyer. Nevertheless, you may be introduced to them by an agent or seller, and you will want to know something about them.

Lease/Option

If you're a first-time buyer who has little to no money for a down payment, you may want to consider this alternative form of financing. It's a pay-as-you-rent way to save money for a down payment. Be aware, however, that it requires a great deal of discipline to make it work.

There is no mortgage involved here. Rather, you and the seller agree on an option-to-purchase plan (detailed in a signed agreement). Under the plan, you agree to *rent* the seller's property for a number of years (usually one to three years). During that time, the payments you make will be divided into two parts. One part will represent rent; the other will represent option money that will go toward a down payment. When you have paid enough money each month to equal a full down payment, you will then obtain a mortgage, and the seller will give you a deed to the property.

For example, you find a condo that you like. Its cost is $90,000, and you need a minimum of $9,000 as a down payment. But you have no money at all to put down.

So, you arrange for a lease/option. Your payment might be $900 a month; $525 of that might go toward rent and $375 toward the down payment. After 24 months, you would have paid the seller $9,000 ($375 X 24) plus rent. At that time, you would exercise the option to purchase and obtain a 90 percent mortgage. The seller would credit you with a $9,000 down payment and you would buy the property.

It can be a good deal for you as a first-time borrower, because it effectively forces you to save the down payment. And usually the amount you pay toward rent is less than market price. For example, the above condo might have a market rental value of $700 a month. But the seller reduces that to $525 to get a future sale. You, on the other hand, pay an extra couple of hundred dollars each month, because you know (or hope) that money is going toward a future down payment.

What you have to be sure of in a lease/option is that you can qualify for a new first mortgage when the option time is up. If you pay for the two years in the above example and then discover you can't qualify for a mortgage, you won't be able to complete the purchase and you'll lose the extra money you've put into the property!

Indeed, while many sellers honestly hope you'll ultimately be able to buy their home, some (particularly highly sophisticated investors) play the lease/option "game." Here they particularly seek out first-time buyers who really don't have a prayer of qualifying for a new mortgage. These unscrupulous sellers are counting on your not being able to qualify for a mortgage and on your not being able to exercise the option. They do it to rake in a couple of hundred extra bucks a month in rent!

You will find many sellers willing to sell on a lease option when the real estate market is down. They can't sell for a cash deal, so they take next best thing, which is the lease/option. In a healthy market, however, you are not likely to find many legitimate sellers offering a lease/option.

It is a good idea to record the lease/option. That way you are assured that the seller can't sell the property to someone else while you're renting and waiting to exercise your option. Be sure to have the owner's signature notarized so the document can be recorded.

Shared-Appreciation Mortgage

This is also a type of mortgage that first-time buyers can use when they have little or no down payment or need a lower down payment. It is a concept that lenders came up with a few years ago when there was rapid appreciation in housing. The lender would offer you a mortgage at a below-market interest rate or with no down payment. In exchange, you would offer the lender an equity position in the property. When you sold, you would split the profits on the sale with the lender.

There are some obvious problems with this. First, what if you don't want to sell? In many cases, loan agreements required you to sell within seven years or so or pay an increased interest rate.

Second, what if the property did not go up in price, as was the case in many areas in the early 1990s? Then neither you nor the lender made any money.

Because of these problems, I know of no shared-appreciation mortgages that are available at this time. The only possible exception has to do with some charitable organizations that are offering shared-appreciation mortgages to first-time buyers or to needy families to purchase and rehabilitate homes in blighted areas in a few large eastern cities.

Reverse Annuity Mortgage

This mortgage is not for first-time buyers but is becoming increasingly popular among the elderly. Here, instead of using the mortgage to purchase a home, it is used as a kind of refinance. The owners remain in the home and, instead of receiving a lump sum, receive so much a month for the remainder of their lives. Each monthly payment increases the mortgage (and the amount of interest to be paid). Eventually, ownership of the home reverts to the lender.

Problems arise when the borrowers live too long and the mortgage begins to exceed the value of the property. Therefore, anyone seeking this type of mortgage needs to have a guarantee behind it. The FHA has been offering this guarantee in a limited number of trial situations.

Buydowns

You may run into this if you're a first-time buyer purchasing a home from a builder. To induce buyers, especially first-time buyers, to purchase new homes, the builder may offer below-market interest rates on financing. For example, the current interest rate may be 9 percent. But the builder, only through its lender, may offer 8 percent. Or it may offer a sliding scale—for example, 6 percent the first year, 7 percent in year two, 8 percent in year three and, finally, the market 9 percent rate the fourth year.

In order to do this, the builder pays the lender the difference between the market rate and the interest rate you are paying. Because the builder pays it up-front all at once, it amounts to less than it would be to you if you had to pay it monthly. But it still usually amounts to thousands of dollars.

Is this a good deal for you? Yes, providing the builder hasn't inflated the price of the home to compensate for the better financing!

Also, if you can afford the current interest rate, you may want to ask the builder to credit you with the money it will cost him for the buydown. For example, if the buydown costs him $5,000, he may be willing to take that much off the price or even to offer it to you as a credit toward the down payment, if your lender will allow this.

Tackling the Long-Awaited Move

CHAPTER  12

Is moving fun? I've moved to a new home, on the average, every three years for the past 30 years. You might say I've become an old hand at it. And while I've gotten to the point where I can say it's quick, efficient and bearable, I can't quite yet say it's fun. You, on the other hand, may see things differently.

It's important to understand that moving into a home for the first time can be quite a bit different from moving between apartments. The items you'll want to bring will be different; timing the move itself can be difficult; and then there's always the matter of hiring a mover versus doing it yourself. (There are some new tax consequences to consider that can have a bearing on this.)

In this chapter we're going to look at the move itself—how to make what is essentially a tense and strenuous situation into something more pleasant. And perhaps we'll find ways to save you money.

WHEN SHOULD YOU PLAN ON MOVING?

Planning the date for the move to your new home can be a bit tricky. Normally, you won't get possession until your new mortgage funds and escrow closes. Then the agent or the seller will hand over the keys and the property will be yours.

But knowing that exact date well in advance is difficult. There are many things that can slow down the sales process. The seller may have a problem with the title, and that could delay the deal. There may be termite or other repair work required, and that could delay things. The lender might have a question or two about your income or credit—another delay. The escrow could lose papers. And on and on.

Occasionally, rarely, a deal will close early. But most of the time there's a problem or two that delays it.

But what if your rent is up on the 30th and you're counting on moving that day? What if that's when all your friends have agreed to come and help? What if that's the date the movers are coming? What if the agent or lender calls a week beforehand and says, "Sorry, we're delayed a few days [or weeks]?"

I think that it's better to be safe and expect delays than to count on things moving like clockwork and be surprised. Perhaps it's a case of Murphy's law—if things can go wrong, they will. Maybe it's just the way real estate deals work. Regardless, if you're a first-time buyer, I suggest you anticipate that the deal won't close on time and you won't get possession on the agreed-upon date. It will probably be later.

How Do You Handle Late Closings?

The important thing here is not to make unbreakable commitments, all of which depend on a particular date. Let's take things one at a time. First, your current home, which I'll assume is an apartment.

Give your landlord notice at least 30 days in advance. (If you have a lease, you are required to continue to rent until the lease term has expired, and the landlord can hold you to this. Usually you have to have a very good reason to break a lease. On the other hand, you could have a nice landlord who will let you out of the lease just for the asking.)

In addition, tell your landlord that you're not sure about the date. You hope it will be the end of the month, but it could be a couple of weeks longer. If it is, will he or she let you pay weekly until you actually have to move?

Some landlords are pretty decent and will go along with you, particularly if you've been renting from them a long time and have been a good tenant. Other landlords think only of the most efficient way to make money, which is to get you out on the 30th and someone else in the next day. Indeed, they may already have a new tenant ready to move in. Usually, however, you can pay an additional full month's rent, if need be, and stay the extra 30 days.

It's important to know in advance which way your landlord is going to handle the situation. If he or she is inflexible, then you may want to make arrangements to temporarily store your furniture and live with a friend (or at a motel). It's not the best of situations, but if you have to, you have to.

You may be tempted to simply leave your furniture in the apartment and not move for a couple of weeks. You figure that it will take a landlord a month or more to evict you and cost a lot of money. And you're moving out anyway, so what do you care?

However, the lender almost always sends a letter to your landlord asking how you've performed as a tenant. Did you always pay your rent on time? Did you ever receive an eviction notice? Landlords have been sufficiently angered by tenants who refused to move when they were supposed to that they called the lender and reported that the tenant/first-time buyer was in default on the rent. That's enough to make a lender hold up on a mortgage, and perhaps even enough to make it refuse to lend!

Anticipate a delay in advance and make contingency plans for it.

When Do You Arrange for Utilities?

I suggest you call the utility companies at least two weeks before the anticipated date of closing. Give them the hoped-for date to turn on the following:

- Phone

- Electricity

- Gas

- Trash disposal

- Cable service

- Any other utility you will use in your area

If you're working with an agent, he or she should provide you with a list of numbers for area utilities. If not, the numbers are often contained in the front pages of the local phone directory. You can also ask the seller what utilities are used. If all else fails, consult the Yellow Pages.

But what if the closing is delayed, as noted above?

I've found that once the utility has your name on its books and has okayed a date for turn-on, it's a simple matter to call up and say, "Hold off turning that on for three days [or a week or whatever]." Utilities are used to such delays and handle them as a matter of course.

What takes time is setting up your account. The utility will probably want time to verify credit information and may even require that you come down and pay a deposit. It can take anywhere from three days to three weeks to initiate service. But once your account is set up, it requires only a phone call to have the turn-on delayed.

WHAT SHOULD YOU ANTICIPATE WHEN YOU FIRST MOVE IN?

If you're renting, you can normally anticipate that the place will be clean and ready to go when you move in. You'll have to do little if any cleanup or repair work yourself. That's not necessarily the case with a home.

Unless you're moving into a new home, you can anticipate that there will be cleaning, painting and more that you will want to do.

You may want or need to put in new carpeting. You may want to do repair work on the kitchen or bathrooms. In short, even though you get possession, you may not want to move in until you first do some work on your new home. Here are some of the things you will want to consider:

❏ *Water heater/furnace turn-on*—The utility company usually won't do this unless you're at home.

❏ *Carpet cleaning*—You can either do this yourself or hire it out. You can rent carpet cleaners at most grocery stores, but don't expect them to do as good a job as professional units.

❏ *Interior cleanup and painting*—Although the house, condo, co-op or townhome may have looked very clean when you saw it with the seller's furniture inside, once the seller moves out, there are always marks and dirt on the walls. Sometimes the ceilings also look bad. You'll probably want to come in and do a lot of cleanup and painting.

❏ *Watering the yard*—Often sellers "forget" to water the last few weeks. Unless you do this immediately, lots of vegetation around the home could die.

❏ *Repair or replacement in kitchen or bath*—You may not like the features of the kitchen or the bathrooms. You may want to put in a new sink or garbage disposal or even a built-in stove. You may want to replace tile in the bathroom.

All of the above tasks take time. What's more, it may be difficult or even impossible for you to live in the house while you're doing them. You may want to live elsewhere for the first few weeks.

Some first-time buyers, therefore, hang onto their apartment for a couple of extra weeks after taking possession of their new home. I know that's paying double rent/mortgage at a time when you're sure to be short of money. On the other hand, it could well be worth a couple of weeks' rent not to have to move and paint and repair all at the same time. (What's it worth to you not to get paint on your couch and stereo?)

What About Broken Items?

After you move in, you may find that certain items just don't work—
the oven doesn't light, or the water heater could be leaking. There
could be an electrical short. It happens, and many times the seller
simply isn't aware of it.

In that situation, you would need to call the agent and the seller
and argue over who should pay to have it fixed—*unless* you have a
home warranty plan. These are offered on almost all homes that are
sold, and usually the seller pays for them (which is a big plus for
you). Under these plans, if there's a problem with almost any system
in the house, the warranty company will come out and fix it, and all
it will cost you is a nominal deductible (usually $35 or $50). If it happens during the first month of ownership, frequently the seller will
be happy to pay the deductible just to avoid any bother.

Ask your agent about a home warranty plan. It should be in your
sales agreement as a condition of sale, if you want the seller to pay
for it.

WILL YOU NEED TO BUY EXTRAS FOR YOUR NEW HOME?

If you've been renting, chances are that the landlord provided a stove,
refrigerator, washer and dryer (even if they were pay-as-you-use-
them items). Most homes, however, come with built-ins, which usually include only the range, oven, garbage disposal and dishwasher.
They do not include a refrigerator or laundry appliances. You will
probably want to buy these things and schedule their arrival for about
the same time as you move in. (Use the same technique here as with
the utility company. Buy well in advance and then delay delivery, if
necessary. Just be sure you can back out of the purchase in case the
home sale falls through.)

You will also probably need a host of other things that renters
frequently don't have, including all sorts of garden tools and so forth.
If the property has a spa or pool, you'll need to buy chlorine, acid,

base, testers, cleaning agents, etc., or arrange for a pool service. (You may also want to take a short course on the care and cleaning of spas and pools.)

There may also be a wide variety of extras such as throw rugs, lamps and additional furniture that you will need. To save money if you're short, a lot of these items, at least for temporary use, can be purchased at thrift shops, Salvation Army stores and so forth. Also, don't forget about garage sales, which are a wonderful source of unusual items.

SHOULD YOU MOVE YOURSELF OR HIRE A MOVER?

I've done it both ways many times, and I can tell you that hiring a mover is best, *if* you have the money. If you're short on money, hiring a moving truck from a rental company can save you bucks, but probably not as much as you may think.

Movers are listed in the Yellow Pages. In having used many, I've found that the quality of the move (whether items get broken or lost) depends more on the individual movers than on the moving company.

Rates are virtually the same and are based on weight. For a certain weight, you'll be charged a certain rate, in most cases, by whichever company you use. Recommendations from people who have recently used movers are helpful; if you get the same company but different people, however, you could get a different result.

There are many moving-truck rental companies, including U-Haul, Ryder, Budget and others. The big differences here are the quality of the equipment and the price. The price varies enormously both from company to company and within a company, which is a big surprise.

I recently moved and hired a mover for the big stuff and a rental truck for the little stuff. I was quoted one price and agreed. However, I had to change the date, and the new price quoted was almost double! By way of explanation, I was told that the price depends on the time of the year, the date of the month and even the day of the week. I had originally wanted to move in the middle of the week in the middle of the month in the middle of summer, the lowest rate period. When I switched to a weekend at the end of the month at the end of summer, I moved to the highest rate period. If I had timed my move a little better, I could have saved a substantial amount of money. It's something to consider when you decide just when you'll move.

From another angle, the amount you pay to rent a truck, plus mileage (if any) plus gas (for a vehicle that may get only a couple of miles to a gallon) may come close to equaling what you would pay a mover to handle the move for you. Try some comparison shopping. You may find that truck rentals cost more and movers cost less than you first thought.

TAX SAVINGS

Many people don't realize that a portion of their moving costs may be deductible from their federal income taxes. It has to do with why you're moving and how far.

If the move is job-related (i.e., you got a new home as part of getting a new job), and if your new home is more than a certain number of miles from your old home (determined by the IRS), you may be able to deduct all of your moving costs up to a maximum amount. You may also be able to deduct some mortgage costs that are not normally deductible.

The rules on this subject change frequently, so check with an accountant to see if they fit you. If they do, you might save enough on your taxes to allow you to afford to hire a mover!

WHAT TO KEEP AND WHAT TO THROW AWAY

Finally, there's the matter of what to save and what to discard when you move. The rule for some people has been throw away nothing, save it all; you can never tell what you will need. For others, it's the opposite: Get rid of everything—whatever you need, you can buy new.

I've found that a good way to determine what to throw away and what to save is to compare the cost of a new item with the cost of moving an old one. For example, a few years ago our family moved about 400 miles. At the time, we had an old washer and dryer. We'd had these units for maybe five years and had originally paid about $350 for both. To buy new ones would cost about $450.

However, because they were heavy, moving them would cost about $150. I argued that it only made sense to move them. If we didn't, we'd spend an additional $300 to buy new.

My wife argued that they were old and we had already gotten our $350 worth of use out of them. It didn't make sense to transport an old washer and dryer 400 miles. There was no sentimental value, and besides, she wanted new appliances.

In the end I prevailed, to my everlasting regret. We moved those blasted appliances 400 miles and installed them in our new home. The trouble was that somewhere along the move, the dryer gave up the ghost. It wouldn't work when we plugged it in. (And moving insurance does *not* pay for internal breakage of appliances and electronics.)

The washer wasn't much better. Within six months it too had to replaced. Thus, because of my stubbornness, we not only had to pay for the $150 move of the two appliances, but we also had to pay another $450 for new ones!

The moral of this story is that if you have old items that will soon need to be replaced and if you have no emotional attachment, dump them. Have a garage sale and get what you can for them. If you can't get anything, haul them off to the dump.

You'll be far better off to be rid of such things than to haul them with you, even if it means popping for the extra money to buy new. This is especially true of anything very heavy, including refrigerators, stoves and worn-out couches.

Moving is always an enlightening (some might even say spiritual) experience. You learn things about yourself (and about your vocabulary) that you didn't know you knew. However, if you take some time to anticipate the problems, it can be much easier. Here's a checklist of what you can do to make your move more fun.

Moving Preparations

❑ Call utilities at least two weeks in advance.

❑ Arrange for a rental truck and/or movers a month in advance.

❑ Give your current landlord at least a month's notice.

❑ Ask your landlord if he or she can be flexible regarding the date you move.

❑ Make specific arrangements for picking up the keys to your new home.

❑ Plan on having overlap time (having two residences for a week or so).

❑ Plan on having time to paint and repair the new place.

❑ Set aside money to cover replacement items (sinks, tile, wallpaper and so on).

❑ Set aside money for new items (washer, dryer, refrigerator, furniture and so on).

❑ Check with your accountant about what parts of the move may be deductible.

❑ Go through your possessions and sell or throw out everything that doesn't have sentimental value or that won't last for a very long time.

❑ Get a good night's sleep before the move and repeat to yourself, "This too will end!"

Capitalizing on Those Tax Benefits

CHAPTER  13

I firmly believe that most people in this country never learn about how taxation really works until they own their first home. Then it comes through in a big way.

Of course, as with most things, there are both pluses and minuses. Here we're going to look at some of the taxing possibilities of first-time home ownership. However, it's important that you don't take this chapter as a guide to doing your own taxes; for that you need a competent accountant, or even a tax lawyer. We're only going to take an overview here so you can see some of the possibilities. You need to check with a professional for your specifics.

I repeat: *Don't use this chapter to help you plan or prepare your taxes.*

THE GOOD THINGS

Of course, there are good things, taxwise, about home ownership. You can still deduct your mortgage interest payments, within certain limitations. The mortgage must be on your principal residence and, if you should be so fortunate as to have one, on a vacation home. (You can deduct the interest on a maximum of two homes.) There are also maximum amount limits.

Deducting Your Mortgage Interest

The maximum mortgage amount on which you can deduct interest as of this writing is $1 million (total, even if you have two homes). This may seem like a lot, and indeed it is; however, Congress in its wisdom has been seeking to dramatically reduce that amount to raise more money for the federal government. It could be far less by this time; so again, check with an accountant.

The mortgage must be for the specific purpose of buying, building or improving a home. This has some interesting ramifications.

If, for example, you decide to get a home equity mortgage and use the money for anything other than improvement or building, you are further limited in how much interest you can deduct. You are limited to a maximum mortgage *for other purposes* of $100,000.

One question that sometimes arises is how much mortgage interest you actually paid during the year. Usually the mortgage lender will send you a statement telling you, so you'll know how much to deduct from your income taxes. But that statement might be inaccurate. For example, normally you would have 12 monthly payments. But what if you paid your January (of the following year) mortgage payment in late December and it was cashed by the lender on December 31? Because interest is paid in arrears (after it's due), you might be entitled to deduct 13 months' interest instead of 12. That could give you a hefty extra deduction and, indeed, many owners do take advantage of it. Check with your accountant to see just how the timing works and how to avoid problems with the IRS if you want to do this.

Deducting Your Property Taxes

In addition, you are also able to take a deduction for the property taxes you pay. We'll get into the trouble with property taxes in a moment, but the good part about them is that they are fully deductible from your income taxes.

Further, they are deductible in the year paid. In most cases, property taxes are payable in December and March. However, if you make both payments in December, you can take the entire deduction in that year—again providing you with another one-time tax deduction boost. This only applies, of course, if you make your own tax payments. If your tax is paid out of an impound (escrow account), then it's normally paid in two installments and you can't take advantage of early payment.

Increasing Your Paycheck Because of Your Interest and Tax Deductions

Because you now have mortgage interest and property tax deductions, you'll owe less federal income tax. You can take home that savings each month by decreasing the number of deductions you take with your employer. Making the calculation, however, can be tricky. You want to get as much as you're entitled to. But if you take too much, you could end up owing more money (and possibly even penalties) on April 15. I suggest you have an accountant or someone who is good with both math and tax rules calculate it specifically for you.

What You Can't Deduct

Some things you can't deduct, however. You can't deduct your insurance payment. Whatever you pay for homeowner's or fire insurance is not of a tax consequence for a principal residence.

You also cannot deduct maintenance of your home. Your bills for gardeners and water simply aren't going to get you a write-off. You also can't deduct the cost of fixing a water heater or repairing the roof, no matter how much they cost.

IMPROVEMENTS ADD TO YOUR BASIS

You can, however, get *some* tax benefit from improvements you make to your home, provided you keep accurate records. To understand how this works, we have to take a step back into the somewhat arcane world of income taxation.

All property, as far as the IRS is concerned, has a "basis." Your basis is usually the price of your home *plus* your costs of purchase, which include closing costs and loan costs not immediately deductible. (We'll cover those shortly.) Your basis is increased by any improvements you make to the property, and that's what we're concerned with here.

For example, let's say you buy a home for $95,000 and your costs of purchase amount to another $3,000. Your basis is now $98,000.

But let's say that you add a room, improve the kitchen and build a fence for a total cost to you of $12,000. Now your basis has jumped to $110,000, as shown below:

Price	$ 95,000
Costs	3,000
Basis	98,000
Improvements	12,000
Adjusted Basis	$110,000

Okay, so you've increased your basis. So what?

The importance of this becomes apparent when it's time to sell. Let's say that you sell your property for $120,000. You sold for more than you paid, so you will have a taxable gain, or profit. How much is it?

Let's assume that it cost you $7,200 in commission plus another $2,800 in closing costs to sell your property, a total of $10,000. When computing gain, you are allowed to adjust the sales price to account for costs, as follows:

Sales price	$120,000
Sales costs	-10,000
Adjusted Sales Price	$110,000

Now comes proof of the importance of keeping track of your improvements. To find your gain, subtract your basis (adjusted for improvements) from your sales price (adjusted for sales costs). It looks like this:

	Before Improvements		*After Improvements*
Adjusted sales price	$110,000		$110,000
Basis	- 100,000	Adjusted basis	- 110,000
Taxable Gain (Profit)	$ 10,000		$ 0

I think you see the picture. By keeping track of all improvements to your property and by using them to raise your basis, you can avoid or reduce the taxable gain when you sell—in other words, save money on your taxes.

What Are Improvements?

Anything that adds value to your property is probably an improvement. It's important to remember, however, that normal repairs and maintenance are not improvements. If you repair a roof, it's not an improvement. If you reseed your front lawn, it's not an improvement. However, if you put on a new, different *and more expensive type* of roof, that might be considered an improvement. And if you put in expensive landscaping, that likewise might be considered an improvement. You should check with an accountant to be sure in your specific instance.

ROLLOVERS

Even if you don't have any improvements to your property, you may still not be liable for taxes when you sell, *if* you roll over the sale of your existing house into another.

This is hardly an issue when you first buy. However, it is very important as a tax-planning tool, and if it's a new concept to you, you should definitely keep it in mind. It works like this. If you buy or build a home that costs more than what you sell your existing home for, any gain (calculated as we've seen above) is deferred into the new home. That doesn't mean the government has overlooked or forgiven any taxes you may owe; it simply means that the payment of those taxes has been put off until sometime in the future. That future time, however, can actually be never. You can continue rolling over your tax liability from your old house into new ones until you die, never paying the tax! (If your new home costs less, you may still be able to defer a portion of the gain.)

There are a few other conditions. You have to purchase the new home within two years before or after you sell the old one, and both homes must be your principal residence. It doesn't work if either is income-producing (rental) property. If, however, you own a duplex and live in one side and rent out the other, then half can be rolled over, and tax must be paid in the year of sale on the other half.

Also, the government is pretty liberal when it comes to deciding what constitutes your principal residence for this rule. It can be your house, condo, co-op, townhouse or even such unusual residences as a motor home in which you live, a mobile home or, in some cases, a boat on which you reside. If you're looking into unusual residences, be sure to check this out.

AFTER YOU REACH THE AGE OF 55— A TAX GIFT!

One of the problems with the rollover rule is that you tend to end up with ever-more-expensive homes. This is fine during your productive career years and while you're raising a family. However, it's a problem when you get older and want to retire. Most of your money may be tied up in a home that's too big, and if you sell and then don't buy a replacement home, you would be liable for that tax you deferred during your lifetime. It could eat up all your profits!

To help avoid this problem, the government allows a once-in-a-lifetime exclusion of up to $125,000. This means that after you reach the age of 55 (if you're married, only one spouse need be 55), you can sell and exclude up to $125,000 of your gain from taxes. That's right, it's yours free—no taxes to pay.

Once again, there are a variety of restrictions. The house must have been your principal residence for the previous three out of five years. (Any combination of three years will do; it doesn't have to be three continuous years.) And you or your spouse can't have taken a previous exclusion. This raises all sorts of issues when it comes to divorce and remarriage, and you may want to get the services of a good tax attorney to help you sort it all out if this is a problem that concerns you.

PAYING THOSE PROPERTY TAXES

Thus far we've been talking almost exclusively about income taxes and your first home. Now let's take just a few moments to consider property taxes.

No matter where you live in the United States, you will be taxed each year on your home. These taxes must be paid, or else the state government, after following tedious procedures, will take the property away from you and sell it to recover the unpaid taxes. Actually, that almost never happens with improved property (land that has a house on it), because your lender, as part of the mortgage agreement you signed, requires you to keep up the property taxes. If you don't pay your taxes, to protect itself, your lender will foreclose. (Lenders actually have a service, which you pay for in your closing costs, that notifies them if at any time the property taxes are unpaid and the state puts a lien on your property.)

This means you can't get away without paying those taxes. But sometimes you can get away with getting those taxes reduced.

Property taxes are called "ad valorem," which means they are levied according to the value of the property. The more valuable your property, the higher the taxes. The lower your property's value, the lower the taxes.

Pay Attention to **Your** *Taxes, Not the Seller's*

This is an important point to keep in mind. The amount of money that the seller pays in taxes on the property may be irrelevant. Your tax bill could be significantly higher.

For example, you're looking at an older home, and the seller is paying only $900 in taxes. That's based on an assessment made years ago. But in your state, property may be reassessed when it is sold. You purchase, and after a month or so an assessor comes out to take a look. He or she determines that the sales price was fair, and now you pay taxes on the new value, which might mean your taxes could be triple what they were.

That's why checking the existing taxes on a property in a state that reassesses upon sale, as some buyers are prone to do, is not only a waste of time but can give you a false sense of what your monthly payments will be. If you're not sure how your state handles property taxes, ask a good agent.

Getting Your Taxes Cut

All it takes to get your taxes cut is to prove that your house isn't worth as much as the state says it is. If you can demonstrate to your local taxing authority that the taxes you owe are unfair because your property has been valued too high, that authority will lower them. The question thus becomes, how do you know if your taxes are too high?

To find out, you need to challenge the tax value placed on your property. Depending on your state, property taxes are reassessed upon sale (as we saw above) or each and every year, or every seven years, or whenever. When it's time to reassess, an assessor will come by to determine the market value. In most states, as noted, it will be at the time you make your purchase.

At that time, it's hard to make a case for a lower market value, because what you paid for the property will determine its value. However, you can argue that you overpaid. The property may be in terrible shape. You may be able to point to half a dozen comparable properties in far better shape than yours that sold for far less. It's not an easy case to make, but it can be done.

You may also challenge the procedure of the assessor. Are the measurements of your lot's and house's square footage right? What about the number of bedrooms and baths? Did the assessor add up all the numbers correctly?

The process of challenging a tax assessment is complex and takes time. Going through the details is beyond the scope of this book. However, a good book to use as a resource is *The Homeowner's Property Tax Relief Kit,* by Lawrence and Vincent Czaplyski (McGraw-Hill, 1993).

GETTING TO KNOW YOUR TAXES

As you can see from this chapter, when you become a homeowner you enter the world of tax planning and legitimate tax avoidance in a rather big way. As a renter, the most you may have done was occasionally adjust your W-4 form, which takes into account your personal deductions. Then maybe you went to the corner tax preparer to get your refund. Unless you were self-employed, that was it.

Now, with a house, there are lots of tax considerations. You may suddenly find that studying the mysterious tax rules of this country can be both an exciting and a potentially profitable way to pass time. If you do, I can suggest a book that may be of use to you. It's called *Tips and Traps for Saving on All Your Real Estate Taxes,* by former USC tax law professor Norman H. Lane and myself (McGraw-Hill, 1994).

Further, you may decide that the tax advantages of owning property are so good that you would like to buy a second house for rental purposes. A great many first-time buyers quickly move on to become first-time landlords. If that's the case, then you will want to check into my book *The Landlord's Trouble Shooter* (Dearborn, 1994).

Tracking Your Annual Profits and Expenses

CHAPTER 14

There are many reasons for buying a home for the first time, as we saw in earlier chapters, but one reason that every first-time buyer acknowledges is the desire to make a profit. It really wouldn't make sense to buy if you expected that several years later you'd sell for a loss. Rather, the hope is that four, five or seven years down the road, or whenever you sell, you'll sell for a lot more money than you paid. Indeed, one of the reasons you probably will decide to sell will be because it's a good time to collect on your investment.

Because a home is such an important investment to the owner, most first-time buyers are eager to keep track of how their investment is doing. After all, if you have a stock or a bond, you watch the paper to see whether it's going up or down. Why should a house be any different?

In fact, tracking home prices has become a kind of game played between owners and real estate agents. You won't be in your property very long before you'll begin receiving unsolicited letters from agents telling you that they've just sold a home in your neighborhood and giving you the selling price. They might even list all recent sales. The idea is to stimulate you into calling them and perhaps listing your home for sale.

I've even been to neighborhood social gatherings where the main topic of discussion was how local home prices were doing. Each neighbor would seem to compete with another to tell a story about a recent sale he or she had heard of.

Of course, as long as prices are going up, everyone feels good. It's when they take a dip that we tend to see lots of glum faces on our neighbors.

I suggest you pick a particular month out of the year—say, December, as it's the year's end and easy to remember. Then each December determine your home's current value. If you're the sort who has accounting blood in you, you might want to plot the price of your home on a graph each year. That way, you can look back and quickly see years when the price didn't seem to move and other years when it shot up (or down).

HOW DO YOU TRACK YOUR HOME'S VALUE?

There are a variety of ways to track your home's value. In this chapter we're going to look at two methods, "on paper" and "in cash." I'm sure you'll find this a fun project, particularly when prices are going up. And it will be helpful to you in that it will let you know how your investment is doing and perhaps signal a good time to sell.

The "On Paper" Method

This is the easiest, and it's what most homeowners use. Unfortunately, it's not very accurate, as we'll see shortly. Nevertheless, it is a good starting point.

What you are going to do is to simply determine how much your home would likely sell for right now. You can use the techniques discussed in Chapter 7 under the heading "How Much Should I Offer?"

Basically, what you need to do is contact a real estate agent and ask for a list of comparable sales going back over the past year. (Because nearly all agents are connected by computers and modems to a central data center, printing this out should take only a few minutes. And any agent will be happy to do this for you hoping that when you do list, you'll call him or her.)

When you get the list, see what homes similar to yours have sold for during the past year. But be careful: Check to be sure you're comparing apples with apples and not with oranges. Be sure the homes have the same number of bedrooms and baths, have the same amenities (such as pools or spas) and are as close to the same number of square feet as possible. Even so, there will still be differences in terms of how fixed up one home is over another, the location on the street and the floor plan. You could, of course, drive by each of the homes to get a better perspective on how similar they really are, but there's no point in being fanatical about this. For the moment, simply taking an average of all recent comparable sales should give you a pretty good idea of what your house should sell for. (Sometimes there are few or even no sales. If that's the case, don't make the mistake of trying to find comparables outside your area. They probably won't really be comparables. You may have to just skip that year's calculation.)

Once you have an average price, subtract two figures from it. The first is how much you paid for your house. The second is how much you owe on your house. That should give you your paper profit and your paper equity.

Calculating the Paper Value

	Profit	*Equity*
Your sales price	$145,000	$145,000
Less purchase price	115,000	
Less current mortgage		90,000
	$ 30,000	$ 55,000

As I said, it's fun to plot this on a graph year to year. You can see how well your real estate investment is doing.

The Cash Method

While the paper method described above gives you a ballpark figure and usually makes you feel good, it's not really a very accurate figure. The reason is that you haven't taken into account the costs you incurred when you purchased your house, nor the costs you will incur when you sell. These can be significant.

You should know your purchase costs from your closing papers. You can estimate your sales expenses as roughly 8 percent of the sales price. That allows for a commission (usually between 5 and 7 percent) and closing costs. It could, however, be more or less.

For the above example, I'm going to assume $6,000 in purchase costs, and 9 percent of a $145,000 sales price is about $13,000 in sales costs. Now the figures look a bit different.

Calculating the Cash Value

		Profit		Equity
Your sales price	$145,000		$145,000	
Less costs of sale	- 13,000		- 13,000	
Adjusted Sales		$132,000		$132,000
Purchase price	$115,000			
Plus buying costs	+ 6,000		+ 6,000	
Current mortgage			90,000	
Adjusted Purchase		- 121,000		- 96,000
Cash		$ 11,000		$ 36,000

After looking at these figures, I'm sure most readers prefer the paper values to the cash values. Unfortunately, in the real world, the cash value is what your property is actually worth and how much you can truly get out of it.

Comparing the Paper and Cash Values

	Profit	*Equity*
Paper	$30,000	$55,000
Cash	11,000	36,000
Difference	$19,000	$19,000

The difference between your profit and your equity on paper and in cash comes to $19,000, a sizable chunk of money. Just remember, the paper price is something to dream about; the cash price is what it's really worth.

Dealing with Buyer's Remorse

CHAPTER

There is a psychological phenomenon that is almost surely going to happen to you as a first-time buyer. Rather than describe it, let me show you what I mean.

You find your first home, and although it may not be perfect, it's close enough to your dream house that you fall in love with it. You and your spouse ooh and aah over all the wonderful features. The master bedroom is large and comfortable and there's a lovely bath off it. The kitchen is cozy, with a window over the sink that looks out over the garden. The garage is big enough for two cars plus any power tools you may purchase. There are extra bedrooms for kids that may be planned in the future. The family room is big enough to accommodate a large-screen TV. It's got wall-to-wall carpeting. It looks like you'll meet lots of friends in the neighborhood, which seems very safe.

So you make an offer, which the seller doesn't accept. But the seller counters, and you counter again, and after some skirmishing, you get the house.

Then it's on to the battle of the lender. Your credit is good, but there are a few problems that you have to explain. The lender wavers, but you finally get a rich aunt to cosign and the loan looks good.

It's going to take all your available cash to come up with the down payment and closing costs, and Lord knows where you'll find the money for the move. But you're going to make it happen.

Then there are the delays. The lender loses a document. The seller discovers there's a lien on the house from an old unpaid bill, and it takes three more days to get that paid off.

Finally, it happens. You put in your money. The lender sends in the mortgage, the seller signs the deed and, miracle of miracles, you own the home!

At last, after all the stretching and pushing and straining, the agent gives you the key, the movers (perhaps a lot of old friends) show up and your furniture somehow gets put into place while you're scrubbing and painting and washing.

What a mess, what stress, what effort. But it's *done!*

REALITY SETS IN

Now it's the first night in your own bed in your new home. You and your spouse are lying there, eyes wide open, thinking about that mortgage. About that BIG mortgage payment. About the huge amount of money you've just paid. About what will happen if you (or if either of you) lose your job.

You begin to sweat, and you say to yourself, "My God, what have I done? Is there any way to get out of this? I want to sell!"

Okay, maybe it didn't happen quite that way. Maybe the panic set in the night the seller signed the sales agreement. Or maybe it was when the lender finally said, "Okay."

But, if you're like the rest of us, at some point—probably totally unexpected—an incredible wave of fear set in. You suddenly realized just how much you had bitten off, and you said to yourself that you just couldn't chew it all.

If this has already happened to you, you know exactly what I mean. If it hasn't yet happened, then read on: I may be able to save you a lot of needless anguish.

This panicky wave of fear has a name. It's called buyer's remorse. It occurs when all the excitement and push and drive to get the new home suddenly wear off, and you're faced with the reality of big mortgage payments and a huge house that you're suddenly not sure you can handle.

I'm not a psychologist and I can't tell you why it happens. But I can tell you it's happened to me and to every first-time buyer I ever knew.

I can also tell you that there's a way to reduce the effect if not eliminate it entirely.

HEALING BUYER'S REMORSE

First, you now have a name for it. Interestingly, once we name things, we seem to gain power over them. Just knowing that it's a phenomenon that frequently occurs can help control it.

Second, you aren't the only one who's on the hook when you buy that home. There's also the lender. You may have put out $5,000 or $10,000 or $20,000 or even more. But that lender put up $100,000 or $200,000 or more. Why are you worrying? Think of how much that lender has to lose!

Further, lenders are not in business to lose money. Most rarely do. They know how to make money on real estate mortgages, and that is to make loans only to people who are qualified to pay them back.

So, if you're suddenly afraid that your judgment has gone bad, rely on that lender's judgment. Remember all those credit checks and documents you brought in? They all proved to the lender that you could indeed make the payments—that you really are qualified to buy this home.

Finally, if the above doesn't help, remember this: It could be worse, far worse. Instead of buying a home, you could be in a country that's at war, with everyone's homes being destroyed. You could have a life-threatening illness. A loved relative or friend could have died.

Buying a home is nothing. You've bought one. Chances are you'll buy others. It's only credit and money. If things don't work out, you can always sell or get rid of the place one way or another. You're not going to be branded for life, and people aren't going to stare at you forever after because you bought this one home.

You're actually starting out on a great adventure. You're taking what may be your first really big step into a wonderful world of investment and accumulating wealth. It's a time for celebrating, not worrying.

So don't be upset with yourself for buying that big house and getting that big mortgage. This too will pass. Think instead of all the good times you'll have in the days to come in your wonderful new home.

INDEX